SUMO

A Pocket Guide

SUMO
A Pocket Guide

by WALTER LONG

photographs by Joel Sackett

CHARLES E. TUTTLE COMPANY

Rutland, Vermont & Tokyo, Japan

The photographer wishes to thank the staff of Olympus Photo Plaza and the Leica distributor in Japan, Nihon Siber Hegner K.K., for their generous technical support and assistance.

Photos on pages 44, 94, and 95 courtesy of Mainichi Shinbunsha *Banzuke* courtesy of the Japan Sumo Association.

Published by the Charles E. Tuttle Co., Inc.
of Rutland, Vermont & Tokyo, Japan
with editorial offices at
2-6 Suido 1-chome, Bunkyo-ku, Tokyo 112

© 1989 by Charles E. Tuttle Co., Inc.
All rights reserved

LCC Card No. 89-50474
ISBN 0-8048-1594-1

First edition, 1989
Third printing, 1991

Printed in Japan

Contents

	Preface	7
1 ·	Three Thousand Years Ago	11
2 ·	Born to Wrestle	18
3 ·	The Long Climb	25
4 ·	Life in the Stables	33
5 ·	Grand Tournaments	39
6 ·	Pageantry, Ritual, and Symbol	61
7 ·	Psychological Warfare	66
8 ·	Sumo Techniques	72
9 ·	The Grand Champions	79
10 ·	Referees and Judges	86
11 ·	What's in a Name?	99
12 ·	The Spoils of Victory	105

13 · The Lure of Sumo	110
Chanko-nabe Restaurants	115
Addresses of Sumo Beya	117
Glossary of Sumo Terms	121

 # Preface

Sumo is a traditional Japanese contest of strength and skill. Its fundamental rules are quite simple: Two men enter a ring and squat, facing each other. On signal from a referee, each tries to best his opponent by forcing him down or out.

Sumo, then, is Japanese wrestling. But to leave it at that is to invite comparison with wrestling in its several Western forms and perhaps to overlook much in sumo that is attractive, exciting, and—as I hope this book will show—occasionally incredible. For sumo is, after all, *Japanese* wrestling, and as with many things Japanese, a superficial simplicity often masks a complex matrix of traditions and values; an innocently decorative object or a slight but precise gesture is often a stand-in for a shared cultural belief or important ritual with roots in antiquity. Thus sumo *is* Japanese wrestling, but at the same time it is something else, something more—a

8 · PREFACE

curious and distinctly Japanese blend of sport and rite, of athletic and aesthetic.

To appreciate sumo, then, it is best to learn something of its history and development. Providing such background information is the concern of the first two chapters of this book. On the other hand, as great a debt as the sport owes to its origins, modern sumo has been adapted and modified to thrive in the twentieth century. It may be a lineal descendant of a bout fought three thousand years ago in China, but it is comprehensible in terms of modern athletic competition. Readers wishing to know only what is happening before them at ringside, or on their television screens (it is broadcast regularly in Japan and Britain; occasionally in the U.S.), may turn to chapters five through eight; these provide a step-by-step explanation of the action during a typical grand tournament. Finally, those curious about the training and daily lives of the competitors, and the people and organizations associated with sumo, will find interesting background material in chapters three and four, and nine through twelve.

A word on sumo terms and their use: The long history of sumo has naturally given rise to a rich specialized vocabulary. Many of these words are introduced and explained, in the belief that readers interested in the sport might like to know some of the terms associated with it. But there is also a practical side to employing them; rather than say or write, for example, that an apparent loser "backed to the edge of the ring and suddenly hoisted and twisted his opponent out," noting a win by *utchari* supplies brevity and precision. On the other hand, a text too larded with Japanese terms is heavy going for readers not familiar with the language. For this reason, accepted English equivalents are alternately and often employed. There are purists who object to this practice, insisting, for example, that a *rikishi* is not really a "wrestler" and that a *dohyo* is not really a "ring." However, even in the West there are many styles of wrestling—hence many different types of wrestlers—and the ring itself turns out to be square. The point is, one must be familiar with a sport to really understand its jargon.

For the reader's convenience, a glossary of all terms used in the text is provided. Although Japanese is widely considered a difficult language, its pronunciation is fairly easy. You will generally be understood if you pronounce every syllable, giving each equal stress, and sound vowels as follows:

a	as in father
i	as in Bali
u	as in true
e	as in press
o	as in colt

As its title indicates, this book is intended as a handy pocket reference, not a comprehensive treatise. More than enough information is supplied to satisfy fans newly won to the sport and those merely curious about it. For those seeking more detailed information, P.L. Cuyler's *Sumo: From Rite to Sport*, is recommended. (I have drawn on this excellent source for much of my brief presentation of the history of sumo.) For those who really wish to follow sumo, more up-to-date information is presented in the magazine *Sumo World*, published in Tokyo one week prior to each of the six annual tournaments (¥650/$4.50 per issue).

No mention has been made of the final, thirteenth chapter of this book, which consists entirely of the author's personal opinion of the merits of sumo. Deficiencies in the reasoning presented there, as well as any errors or omissions in any part of the text, are entirely his responsibility, and are not to be charged to his sources, his publisher, or the Japan Sumo Association.

CHAPTER 1

Three Thousand Years Ago

Contests of physical strength were an early development in many ancient cultures. Thus there is no reason to suppose that sumo is not an indigenous Japanese sport. However, it is probable that the native Japanese form of wrestling was subject to the influence of mainland Asian wrestling styles. Various forms of wrestling were presented as royal entertainments in China as early as the Western Zhou dynasty (beginning around the eleventh century B.C.). And Korean tomb paintings from the sixth century, a time when Chinese influence on Japan via Korea was particularly strong, depict loincloth-clad wrestlers very similar to those portrayed in Japanese tombs of later date. An accurate picture of the development of Japanese wrestling, however, will likely not emerge until the origins of the Japanese people themselves become clearer.

One of the earliest Chinese forms of wrestling was

called *jiao-li*, meaning "horned power." In these contests, wrestlers wearing horned masks would try to butt each other into submission in a ceremony that took place during rural agricultural festivals. Western Zhou people followed a primitive but complex system of nature worship in which animals figured prominently. This is evidenced by the dynasty's amazing legacy of bronze vessels, which portray a wide variety of ordinary and fantastic creatures; these vessels were used in rituals—often involving live animal sacrifices—to appease the powers ruling the Zhou cosmos. It is likely that *jiao-li* contests were held as entertainments for the gods—as a way of capturing their attention and winning their favor. With the unification of China in the third century B.C., the kingdom's rulers began to assume a role grander than that of mere temporal authority. They were "sons of heaven," intermediaries between the realms of god and man. Thus it was logical that wrestling should develop into an imperial entertainment, a fact attested to in Chinese dynastic histories.

The linkage of sport and rite is also evident in early Japanese wrestling, again, not necessarily as a result of Chinese influence. In Japan, sumo was and is closely associated with Shinto, which is usually translated as "the way of the gods." Shinto is an indigenous Japanese system of nature worship. It posits myriad *kami*, or deities, resident in or associated with both animate and inanimate objects. Appeasement of *kami*, through acts of ritual purification or properly enacted ceremonial, is deemed essential to the maintenance of a harmonious relationship between man and nature. The public face of Shinto is most evident in the *matsuri*, or festivals, which are held to promote or celebrate planting, fertility, and bountiful harvests—concerns vital to those dependent upon the agricultural cycle. *Matsuri* are an occasion for both reverence and revelry—*kami* are to be respected but must also be entertained. And part of the entertainment was often *shinji-zumo*, literally "god-service sumo." Shinto-related *matsuri* that incorporate sumo as part of the festivities are still common in many parts of Japan.

The emperors and empresses of Japan have traditionally been considered lineal descendants of Shinto's principal deity, Amaterasu, the Goddess of the Sun. As such, they have played an important role in Shinto ritual, performing—or sending imperial messengers to witness—the important rituals marking the agricultural calendar. The emperor traditionally plants the first rice seedlings in the spring and offers the first fruits of the grain harvest at the Grand Shrines of Ise in the fall. Thus, god-service sumo and nonreligious sumo, although deriving from separate traditions with ostensibly different purposes, were never entirely distinct. As in the Chinese tradition, the overlapping of the functions of appeasement of the gods and imperial entertainment was natural one. Nonreligious sumo, from which modern sumo is derived, was to receive a tremendous boost during later periods of civil war through its new function as a military art. But it would never divest itself entirely of its strong Shinto associations.

Sumo remained popular with the court throughout

the Heian period (794-1185). During the early part of this period, the emperor had authority in name only; the government was actually run by members of the powerful Fujiwara clan. The court consequently had much free time to devote to ritual and ceremonial activities. The Heian period was a high point in Japanese culture, and the lavishness of its pageantry rivaled that of the contemporary Tang dynasty in China. Sumo thrived; it was ranked with archery and equestrian archery as one of the three sports for which great ceremonial competitions were held annually. A Bureau of Champions was even established to scout good wrestling prospects from the provinces.

By the latter half of the Heian period, however, two great warring clans—the Minamoto and Taira—had arisen; the country was plunged into an extended period of warfare as the two struggled for control. Sumo no longer held a strictly ceremonial function, but was beginning to be considered a military art, the proper use of which was in the service of one of the many contending warlords. In feudal Japan, victory in battle was often determined by the outcome of a contest between individual samurai, and sumo—along with archery and swordsmanship—was one of the martial skills employed to determine a winner. It remained a form of entertainment as well, however, for soldiers would often hold impromptu bouts when encamped, to relieve the boredom of campaigning.

In an era of incessant warfare, martial games were naturally encouraged by the nobility. Contests of wrestling, archery, and horseracing were frequently held, most often, naturally, at shrines and temples during festivals; thus the strong association of sumo with religious rite was maintained.

By the end of the sixteenth century, guns had been introduced into Japan by the Portuguese, severely limiting the efficacy of wrestling skills on the battlefield. And there were also, of course, extended periods of peace. Both these factors helped to promote the appearance of masterless samurai-wrestlers. As did their more famous counterparts, the masterless samurai-swordsmen, these fighters would roam the country in search of bouts with local champions. They could earn a living by appearing in regional tournaments, in which purses were offered to participants or winners. Many such contests were held to raise money for the construction of roads and bridges, or for the support of shrines or temples; they were referred to as *kanjin-zumo*, or "benefit sumo."

As the seventeenth century opened, the powerful lord Tokugawa Ieyasu was eliminating the last of his rivals and consolidating his control of the country. The first shogun of a line that would last until imperial power was restored in 1868, Ieyasu controlled the government from his military headquarters at Edo, now known as Tokyo, although the emperor still held court at Kyoto. It was a time of great social transformation in Japan, one which saw a huge increase in commercial activity and with it the rise of a commercial culture. Watching sumo, attending kabuki performances, and wining, dining, and dallying in the gay quarters became the favored pastimes of the new merchant class. And the ruin of many great feudal houses had assured a ready supply of masterless samurai anxious to win money, fame, and perhaps a new patron in organized benefit-sumo tournaments or even in pickup bouts called *tsuji-zumo*, or "street-corner sumo."

Early Edo was a tough town, however, and these contests were nothing like the stately ceremonial affairs of Heian times. They were often just brawls that resulted in escalating violence, swordplay, and death. To check these problems, both street-corner sumo and benefit sumo were outlawed in 1648 for a brief period, and in 1661 all forms of sumo were banned from Edo. The proscription lasted until 1684, when one Ikazuchi Gondaiyu successfully petitioned authorities for permission to stage a benefit-sumo tournament. To win the concession, Gondaiyu had to formulate and present an elaborate set of rules and regulations designed to lessen the possibility of violence. These included, for the first time, specifications regarding the ring, and the holds and throws that could be legally used. A bloodless—hence successful—tournament resulted, leading to the scheduling of more such regulated events, in Osaka and Kyoto as well as Edo. Professional groups of wrestlers were formed, who would plan, promote, and stage regular tournaments. In Edo, these began to be held regularly, in the third and tenth months of the lunar year. The increasing systematization and codification would ultimately, after much trial and error, result in the organized, highly regulated sport that is sumo today.

That, in brief, is the three-thousand-year history

of a professional sport that you may view today on television. But a recitation of the origins and development of sumo is a rather dry affair without a look at some of the colorful personalities and interesting anecdotes associated with it, the subject of the next chapter.

CHAPTER 2

Born to Wrestle

Given its ancient roots, there has naturally accrued to sumo a great deal of lore and legend—odd anecdotes involving colorful characters.

The first recorded sumo bout was a rather straightforward affair, fought at the request of Emperor Suinin around 23 B.C. This fight pitted the formidable wrestler Taima-no-Kehaya against Nomi-no-Sukune, who supposedly stood seven feet ten inches tall. After a long, pitched battle that reportedly thrilled the audience, Sukune dealt Kehaya a powerful, well-placed kick that broke his ribs and killed him on the spot. The property of the loser was seized and given to Sukune, who was also awarded a position as a retainer of the emperor. The story of this bout is told in the *Kojiki (Records of Ancient Matters)*, the earliest Japanese history, written about 712 B.C. Shrines to both of these wrestlers can be found in the former land of Yamato, that part of western Japan ruled by Suinin and his descendants.

A thirteenth-century text chronicles an instance of the imperial succession being decided by the outcome of a sumo bout. When Emperor Montoku announced his intention to retire in 858 B.C., the throne was claimed by both his eldest son, Koretaka, and his fourth son, Korehito. The emperor decreed that the matter would be settled by a sumo match, and wrestlers were chosen to represent each side. The eldest son was championed by a powerful-looking giant named Natora, while the wrestler representing Korehito was a scrawny little fellow named Yoshio. Unknown to all, however, the most important player in the drama was a Buddhist monk, who sat at ringside praying fervently for a miracle. As the bout opened, Yoshio was mauled by his bigger opponent, and appeared a sure loser. Just then, however, a huge water buffalo wandered along. As it approached, Natora's strength seemed gradually to be sapped, while Yoshio appeared to grow stronger. Of course, Yoshio won the bout, and Korehito became the emperor Seiwa, ruling until 876.

Sumo wrestlers are, and in the main always have been, men. But there have been some interesting exceptions. At a benefit-sumo tournament held in Kyoto in 594, for example, victory seemed all but assured for a wrestler called Tateishi. After Tateishi had beaten all his opponents, the referee stepped forward and called out to the crowd for more challengers. It appeared that no one was going to respond when up stepped a young nun. Tateishi at first refused to fight, but the audience was so amused, he figured he would play along with the jest. As the nun moved toward him, he simply stood with his arms spread. But when she began to actually push him backward, he was horrified, and began to wrestle in earnest. When he crouched and grabbed for her arm, however, she took hold of his thigh and threw him to the ground. The crowd went wild. Tateishi was mortified, but his embarrassment was somewhat mitigated when she threw the next three challengers. The wrestling nun later appeared in several more tournaments, always winning.

In the Edo period, bouts were actually held between women wrestlers. These were not really displays of martial skill, but reflected the sport's growing role as a popular entertainment—the women's mud wrestling of the day. The wrestlers themselves were not much to look at, if contemporary prints are any reliable guide, but they had suggestive names, like Chichigahari, or "Big Tits," and Anagafuchi, or "Deep Trench." For the crowd's amusement, the women were often matched against blind men, leading to much groping and grabbing.

On the more serious side, sumo wrestlers have figured in some important political transitions, and not only of the legendary kind related above. A group of wrestlers participated in the taking of Shimonoseki during the Choshu Civil War of 1865. Their successful resistance against the forces of the Tokugawa shogunate contributed significantly to the eventual restoration to power of the Meiji emperor in 1868, an event that heralded Japan's drive to modernization.

Modern sumo wrestlers are called *rikishi*, literally

"strong warrior," a term that dates from the early eighteenth century. (Another general name for sumo wrestlers, *sumotori*, is now more often used to denote wrestlers in the lower divisions.) Whereas *rikishi* formerly came from the ranks of the samurai, the warrior class of feudal Japan, today's wrestlers are more likely to be sons of farming or fishing families. A disproportionate number of them hail from northern Japan, particularly the great island of Hokkaido. As a matter of fact, the three reigning grand champions, of whom we will learn more in chapter nine, are all from Hokkaido. One reason for this, it has been suggested, is that trudging through the heavy snows that blanket northern Japan during the winter strengthens the hips and legs.

There may be some merit to this argument. To avoid being toppled, a *rikishi's* center of gravity should be as low as possible. A "natural" wrestler, then, has relatively short legs with wide hips and well-developed thighs, and a longish, less well-developed upper torso with long arms. The weight and stability of his lower body makes him difficult to move or throw, while with his long arms and torso he can go after his opponent's belt—an effective tactic—while keeping him at a distance. Life in Japan's snow country could certainly produce such a physique. But this explanation does not account for the great number of wrestlers who come from Kyushu, Japan's southern main island, which sees little snow.

Nor does it account for the increasing numbers of foreigners in sumo. Japanese society has been described as being for the most part closed to foreigners, and the tightly knit world of sumo has been even more so. In 1885, the request of an American to join the sport was refused. Shortly after World War II, however, an American-born Japanese who had been passing himself off as a native reached the top division of sumo. And a few years after that, he was joined by a Japanese-born Korean named Rikidozan.

Quite a colorful character, Rikidozan abruptly quit sumo in 1950. As one of his reasons for leaving, he charged that, as a foreigner, he was not allowed to advance to the rank of grand champion; however, it is likely that monetary difficulties subsequent to a prolonged illness played the biggest role in his decision to quit. Rikidozan then shocked the sumo world by going into pro wrestling, a sport as theatrically absurd and low-class in Japan as it is in the West. He became quite popular and successful, however, and later retired to manage a number of nightclubs. In one of these he was stabbed to death by a gangster in 1963.

As Japan has become more prosperous and international in outlook, the world of sumo has also opened up a bit. Koreans, Chinese, Brazilians, Tongans, and mainland Americans have all tried their hand at it. Most have given up and returned home, not due to any overt discrimination, but simply because, as we shall see, the life of a novice wrestler is a difficult one. However, some foreigners have been successful, most notably the Hawaiian *rikishi* Takamiyama (formerly Jesse Kuhaulua), who retired in 1984.

Jesse, as he is popularly known, entered sumo in 1964, when he was nineteen years old. Four years later he arrived in the top division of sumo, and four years after that became the first foreigner ever to win a grand tournament. During the awards presentation following his victory, the American ambassador to Japan read him a congratulatory telegram from President Richard Nixon. An amiable bear of a man, Jesse was, and still is, widely popular. He never achieved the rank of grand champion, but managed to spend twenty years in sumo. His amazing durability resulted in several records: for the most consecutive tournament appearances in the top division, 97; for the most career bouts, 1,654 (a record since surpassed by Oshio); and for the most consecutive top-division bouts, 1,231. He also holds a record number of twelve *kinboshi*, "gold stars" awarded for beating grand champions. He became a Japanese citizen in 1980 and opened a sumo training gym under the name Azumazeki when he retired.

In spite of Jesse's success, however, the world of sumo remains conservative and nationalistic. When a newcomer from abroad moves up the ranks with unseemly ease, as did the current top-ranking foreign wrestler, Konishiki, the question of whether foreign participation in sumo should be barred or restricted is debated anew.

From wherever they hail, aspiring *rikishi* must be of a minimum height and weight. These standards have been raised gradually over the years, as the increasing protein content of the Japanese diet has produced successively taller and more massive generations. Today, young men who desire to join sumo must stand at least five feet eight and weigh 165 pounds.

Considering the size of the top-ranked *rikishi*, these standards seem very minimum indeed. For even taking into account legendary giants, the biggest men in sumo history are those wrestling today. The heaviest of them is Konishiki, who tips the scales at about 560 pounds (enough weight for more than three applicants!). Since he hails from Hawaii, however, Konishiki (real name Salevaa Atisanoe) cannot be offered as evidence of the increasing bulk of the Japanese. That role might fall to the present grand champion Onokuni, who stands six feet two-and-a-half inches and weighs 448 pounds.

Obviously, then, most of the *rikishi's* bulk results from the diet and training regimen that he undertakes after entering sumo. These and other aspects of the newcomer's long and difficult struggle to the top are the subjects of chapters three and four.

CHAPTER 3

The Long Climb

A new wrestler enters sumo by becoming affiliated with a training facility called a *beya*, a term popularly, if inelegantly, translated "stable." Most *beya* are located near Ryogoku Station on the JR Sobu Line, for it was in this area that the first national sumo stadium, the Kokugikan, was constructed in 1909. There are about a dozen *beya* clustered about the third and newest Kokugikan, which opened in 1985 in the same vicinity, and around forty altogether (a list of *beya* addresses appears on pages 117–19). Most *beya* are not particulary attractive—just ordinary wood-frame or concrete houses, each containing little more than a ring, a communal eatery, and some rather spartan sleeping quarters.

The young hopeful must pass a physical examination, held six times a year (before each of the major tournaments), and present the required documents (parental consent and a copy of the family register). He is then formally enrolled as an apprentice wrestler, becoming for all practical purposes the property of the Japan Sumo Association. The newcomer might be a strapping farm boy or a fisherman's son with little training in the sport, or a veteran college wrestler. But in any case, he has a long and difficult climb ahead of him. For these *beya* house altogether about 800 wrestlers, and all are competing with one another in the struggle upward through a rigid system of ranks.

Ascending through the sumo hierarchy is somewhat like climbing a mountain. Progress is rather quick and painless at its broad base—the entry level—but becomes progressively slower and more difficult as one approaches the steep and slippery summit. As a matter of fact, the word *nobori*, "to climb," is a popular suffix for a wrestler's name; it gives notice of his intention to climb to the summit of the sumo world.

There are six major divisions in sumo. These are best considered as falling into two groups—the base and summit of our figurative mountain—for there is a wide disparity in the prestige and privileges accorded members of each group. The base consists of the four lower divisions; they are (from the bottom up): the *jonokuchi* division, with about 100 wrestlers; the *jonidan* division, with about 300; the *sandanme* division, with about 200; and the *makushita* division, fixed at 120 wrestlers. Although the numbers of wrestlers in the divisions below *makushita* vary, a little arithmetic reveals that this leaves only sixty-odd slots in the top two divisions—a precipitous summit indeed.

A novice wrestler, as a matter of fact, does not really

begin to climb the mountain right away; he is only allowed to view it from a distance as he hikes toward it. For although he is officially a member of the sumo world, his bouts are considered *mae-zumo*, literally "pre-sumo" and his name will not appear on the *banzuke*, the official list of participants in a tournament. *Mae-zumo* bouts are held early in the morning during grand tournaments. The novice needs three wins (three "white stars") to graduate from *mae-zumo*; he is allowed to keep trying, at a pace of one bout per day, until he succeeds. This test passed, the newcomer is ready to begin his climb in earnest. He will be presented to the public in a special ceremony. In the next tournament, his name will appear on the *banzuke*—in tiny letters at the bottom, of course, but designating him a full-fledged contender for the championship of his division.

There are exceptions to these procedures. Experienced college wrestlers are placed at the bottom of the *makushita* division, bypassing *mae-zumo* and the lowest ranks. And at Osaka tournaments additional *mae-zumo* bouts are held, to increase chances for the many aspirants to a sumo career.

The next division of sumo is the *juryo*, which is topped by the highest division, the *makunouchi*. The former takes its name from an old Japanese coin called a *ryo*; ten *ryo* (or *ju ryo*,) was the salary of wrestlers of that rank. The *juryo* division has twenty-six wrestlers, the *makunouchi* thirty-six to thirty-eight (depending upon how many wrestlers are holding titles). These numbers vary only slightly—an addition to their ranks depends on someone dropping out or being demoted.

Wrestlers in these top two divisions are referred to as *sekitori*, literally "to capture the barrier," a carry-over, it is said, from the days when wrestlers were samurai and thus actively took part in military offensives. Attainment of *sekitori* rank brings with it a huge leap in status; more than any other promotion, save perhaps to *yokozuna*, it is the mark of success in a sumo career.

Sekitori status is evident from a wrestler's apparel and hair style. All *rikishi* let their hair grow when they enter sumo. It is tied in a simple topknot called a *chon-mage* and is kept in place with a scented pomade called *bin-tsuke*. For tournaments and other formal occasions, *sekitori* sport a more elaborate style called *o-icho-mage*. For this style the hair is pulled back, gathered, and then fanned out in the shape of a ginkgo leaf.

Rank can also be determined from the quality of a *rikishi's* belt, called a *mawashi*. It is made from about thirty feet of cloth, folded lengthwise a number of times, passed between the legs and then wrapped around the waist. *Rikishi* practice in *mawashi* of cotton canvas, black for *sumotori*, white for *sekitori*. For tournaments, *sekitori* switch to *mawashi* of pure silk, often in bright colors, while lower-division wrestlers must make do with their practice belts. All wrestlers during tournaments wear tucked into the front of their *mawashi* a thin band called a *sagari*, from which hang a number of twisted and stiffened silk cords.

Sumo may be rigidly structured but it is eminently fair. Advancement through the ranks comes through winning tournament bouts, and thus depends entirely on the wrestler. *Rikishi* are re-ranked following each

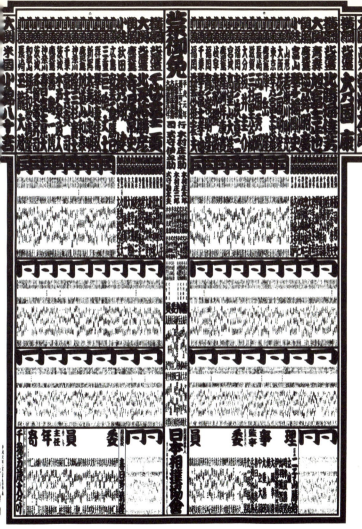

A *banzuke*, the official list of tournament participants.

tournament on the basis of their performance. Since sumo has no weight classes—all *rikishi* are theoretically heavyweights—this method of re-ranking ensures that wrestlers will for the most part be matched against opponents of similar power and ability. A wrestler who achieves a majority of wins, or *kachi-koshi,* will be promoted; one who records more losses than wins, or *make-koshi,* will be demoted. The degree of promotion or demotion is in proportion to the won-lost record.

Rikishi do not wrestle more than once a day during tournaments. Those in the lower ranks participate in only seven bouts; *sekitori* enter fifteen bouts. With only seven bouts per tournament, it takes time for a lower-ranking *rikishi* to work his way up to the top two divisions; five to seven years has been considered average. However, since there are more grand tournaments now than there were in the past, and since college wrestlers bypass the lowest divisions, it is now possible to advance through the ranks with greater speed. About a half dozen of the top *sekitori* now wrestling won promotion to *makunouchi* within two years after entering sumo. But these are exceptions, and there are several who took more than ten years.

Makunouchi means "inside the curtain," from the days when *rikishi* sat on a curtained-off platform awaiting their bouts. The thirty-eight wrestlers of this division are further divided into several subgroups and ranks. At the bottom are the *maegashira* (literally "before the head") wrestlers, who are ranked by number, from *maegashira* one (the highest) through thirteen or fourteen. (On the *banzuke,* the *maegashira* designation continues through the *juryo* division.) Two wrestlers share each designation, one representing the position for the east, one for the west. This traditional division of contenders into two sides originally had some geographical or team basis, but now serves merely as a convenient method of organizing rankings and tournament bouts.

The difficulty of becoming a member of the elite *makunouchi* group is readily evident from the numbers: Its *rikishi* total, after all, less than five percent of all wrestlers active in the sport. Moreover, not even a *makunouchi* wrestler can rest on his laurels. Since his rank is re-evaluated after each tournament, he may bounce up and down within (or even in and out of) the division. It often happens that a wrestler, after a particularly successful tournament, wins promotion to a high ranking that is really beyond his capabilities to hold. Meeting mostly top men in the next tournament, he compiles a dismal record, which sends him down into the ranks of wrestlers far less capable than he. So he trounces them all in the next tournament and shoots to the top again. Such wrestlers are popularly referred to as "elevator *rikishi*."

Above the *maegashira* are the *sanyaku*, the three ranks of "ordinary" titleholders. The highest of these is the *ozeki*, or "champion," followed by a *sekiwake*, sometimes called "junior champion, first class," and *komusubi*, or "junior champion, second class." There are two each of the *sekiwake* and *komusubi*, one each on the east and west sides, and anywhere from two to four *ozeki*, two apiece for each side. The two lower-grade titleholders are subject to the same rules for promotion and demotion as the other wrestlers, but the *ozeki* are given a break: They will not be demoted unless they fail to make *kachi-koshi* in two successive tournaments. *Ozeki* literally means "great barrier," which in the sumo world it truly is; only about one in 500 wrestlers attains this rank.

Finally, above the *sanyaku*—literally the "three ranks"—are the *yokozuna*, or "grand champions," who stand at the pinnacle of sumo. Subject neither to promotion nor demotion, however, *yokozuna* are in a class, and hence a chapter, by themselves.

CHAPTER 4

Life in the Stables

Although feudalism supposedly came to an end in Japan in 1868, some say it is alive and thriving in the institution of the sumo *beya*. Having sworn fealty to his new lord, the stablemaster, the aspiring *rikishi* does whatever he is told to do. He may be assigned as a cook, janitor, or *tsukebito*—an "attendant" to a *sekitori* or a coach. He will take on the dirtiest and most menial chores of the *beya*, in return for which he will receive only the necessities of life and the chance to advance. Meanwhile, he will take his place at the bottom of a rigid hierarchy—the first whenever there is work to be done and last whenever it is time to eat or relax.

Warm-up exercises and practice in the *beya* are also undertaken in order of rank, lowest to highest. Novices must rise early, around half-past five, to get started with their workouts, while the senior *rikishi* sleep in until a more reasonable hour. There is no breakfast, nor eating or drinking of any kind before practice. New wrestlers must attend a sort of sumo boot camp, held at the Kokugikan. There they go through a grueling daily workout and learn the basic techniques, including how to fall—safely, if not gracefully. They also study the history and traditions of sumo and practice enough calligraphy to be able to sign an elegant autograph. (Elocution is apparently not a part of this program, for no one is more terse and shy than a *rikishi* being interviewed on TV after an important win.) Following six months of this basic indoctrination, the newcomers will begin to train with their stablemates.

Many of sumo's basic exercises and training routines are unique to the sport. *Rikishi* practice a variety of movements designed to stretch and loosen the muscles, including what are called *shiko* and *matawari*. The former is performed by lifting a leg straight and high into the air, then slamming the foot to the ground. The hard thumping has a symbolic significance and figures prominently in the pre-bout ceremony at tournaments; here its purpose is to loosen and strengthen the muscles and joints of the hips and legs. *Matawari* is sometimes translated "sumo splits"; seated on the ground with each leg extended as straight out to the side as possible, the *rikishi* bends over until his upper body touches the ground. The younger wrestlers often cannot attain this painful-looking position, and are helped by senior *rikishi* who push down on their backs. Another exercise certainly found only in sumo is *teppo*, the slapping of a wooden pillar with the open hands, one after the other. This is performed in conjunction with sweeping foot motions to help coordinate arm and leg movement. *Shiko* and *teppo* are normally performed before practice bouts; *matawari* is performed after.

Training of all types is referred to as *keiko* (pronounced *geiko* as a suffix). The first type of the day is usually *moshiai-geiko*, a kind of "King of the Mountain" played in the practice ring. Two lower-ranked wrestlers square off and fight, with the winner choosing the next challenger, and so on. Obviously, wrestlers who win get more practice and, theoretically at least, get better. The shaking-out process thus begins at the lowest levels of the sport. All of the training is carefully watched, either by the *beya* coaches or the stablemaster himself (who is addressed as *oyakata*, a term that applies to all elders of the Japan Sumo Association). A *rikishi* who does not display the proper enthusiasm or energy will find his instruction punctuated with the sharp rap of a broom handle or bamboo stick. Each level of practice concludes with a session of *butsukari-geiko*. This pits a larger, senior wrestler against one of smaller stature and rank, who charges across the *dohyo* and tries to push him out. Each of the younger *rikishi* gets a chance to take on a senior stablemate.

As the morning progresses, *rikishi* of progressively higher divisions take their turns in the ring, and then move off to perform their winding down exercises elsewhere, followed usually by chores. Around eight o'clock or so, the *sekitori* make their appearance. They begin their training bouts around nine, when the younger wrestlers return to watch and assist. At this time, another form of training, *sanban-geiko*, may be undertaken. This consists of the same two men fighting multiple, successive bouts; it is both a test of endurance and a chance to hone technical skills. *Sanban-geiko* often takes place between *rikishi* of different divisions, and thus provides an excellent training opportunity for the lower-ranked men. Higher-ranked *rikishi* try at all times to help out their juniors. The assistance may be in the form of a little extra instruction in technique, or a sudden and solid whack called *kawaigatte*, literally "treating with affection." Training concludes before noon, usually with exercises and a short period of meditation. Before tournaments, *rikishi* often train with wrestlers from a neighboring *beya*. Called *de-geiko*, or "outside training," it allows *rikishi* to engage in practice bouts with opponents they may actually meet in competition.

While the *sekitori* are practicing, the first and main meal of the day is being prepared in the kitchen by the junior wrestlers and, if the *beya* is lucky enough to have one, a full-time chef. Before eating, the *sekitori* file off to their baths, which also have been prepared by the junior wrestlers. The *tsukebito* scrub down the backs of their assigned seniors, who then head off to lunch. The junior wrestlers must content themselves with tepid bath water and the leftovers from the noon meal.

The main dish at this meal is the famous *chanko-nabe*, a stew consisting of some type of meat or fish cooked with a variety of vegetables in a broth. Spinach, onion, carrots, *daikon* (a large, long white radish), Chinese cabbage, and *shiitake* (Japanese mushrooms) are a few of the vegetables used, and *tofu* (soybean curd) is usually added. Eaten with several side dishes and many bowls of white rice, and washed down with beer and saké, this high-carbohydrate meal is calculated to put on weight, especially when followed by a mandatory nap of several hours.

Afternoons at the stable are fairly quiet. Married wrestlers who live at home are allowed to leave after the noon meal, while the younger wrestlers still have many errands to run elsewhere. Unmarried *sekitori* may use the afternoon to take care of fans' requests for *tegata*—autographed palm prints—or they may simply rest before evening social obligations. For as with other heroes in the public eye, they are in great demand to appear for worthy civic or charity causes, as well as to promote business ventures. In addition, they must satisfy the demands of their fans and supporters. While they are out being wined and dined, the junior *rikishi* have their meal in the *beya*, usually a simple affair.

As noted in the previous chapter, a quantum jump in privilege and prestige comes with the attainment of *sekitori* status—membership in one of the top two divisions, the *juryo* and *makunouchi*. Promotion to *juryo* rank essentially marks an end to a wrestler's service to others; in the future, he will be served. He will be assigned a *tsukebito*, who will run errands for him, answer his phone, and assist him in bathing and dressing. He may now get married and live away from the *beya*; while he remains a bachelor, he will be given a private room.

The new *sekitori* must also be supplied with accouterments befitting his new status. He will need the elaborately embroidered apron called a *kesho-mawashi*, which is worn in the ring-entering ceremony. This is usually presented by the stable's *koen-kai* (supporters group or fan club); another may be presented later by the new *sekitori's* own *koen-kai*, which he is now entitled to have. He will be given a new *mawashi* of silk, for use in tournaments, and a lacquered wickerware trunk, an *akeni*, in which his *tsukebito* will carry all this new equipment to and from tournaments.

All in all, life for the new *sekitori* will become much pleasanter, although, in truth, he will have more work to do—for he will now wrestle on all fifteen days of tournaments instead of on only seven. On the other hand, he will finally get paid for his work—only *sekitori* receive regular salaries.

CHAPTER 5

Grand Tournaments

Unlike many other sports, sumo does not have a season. It takes place throughout the year, and there is no regular competition that culminates in a post-season championship contest like a Super Bowl or World Series. Or perhaps it would be more accurate to say that each of the six fifteen-day sumo tournaments held each year is a complete season in itself, for in each a series of bouts culminates in the matching of *rikishi* with the best records, one of whom will be declared the tournament winner.

Sumo tournaments are called *basho*, meaning "place" or "site," a word that is added as a suffix to tournament times and locations. As we have seen, by the middle of the seventeenth century the sport had become quite popular in the new capital of Edo (now Tokyo) and tournaments were beginning to be held regularly. They took place outdoors, in specially constructed arenas on the grounds of shrines or temples. Patrons could sit on mats in roped-off boxes at the ground level, or in tiered balconies, which could be reached by means of bamboo ladders. These complexes were surrounded by high wooden walls to keep out freeloaders, and tea houses were set up nearby to cater to the needs of the patrons.

About this time, the list of tournament contenders, the *banzuke*, began to take on its modern form. A one-page program for a 1757 tournament for the first time listed wrestlers vertically in order of rank, in two rows, east and west. A later refinement was the listing of *rikishi* in progressively larger characters as their rank increased. This had two obvious advantages: Status-conscious Japanese could see at a glance who were the top *rikishi*, and the names of lower-ranked wrestlers, who were far more numerous than those in the upper ranks, could all be squeezed onto a single page. This format is almost exactly that used today. (Incidentally, *banzuke* make handy and inexpensive souvenirs. They can be purchased for ¥50 each at the offices of the Japan Sumo Association in the Kokugikan beginning thirteen days prior to all *basho*.)

Sumo remained a biannual Tokyo event throughout the Meiji and Taisho periods (1868–1926), though up to 1925 there was a separate sumo organization operating in Osaka. Additional *basho* were added in the 1940s and 50s in response to the sport's increasing popularity and the desire of fans in other parts of Japan to see it live. In 1953, an Osaka tournament and a third Tokyo tournament were officially added; another, in Fukuoka, on Japan's southern island of Kyushu, was established

At 450 pounds, Onokuni is the heaviest Japanese sumo wrestler, or *rikishi*, in the history of the sport *(right)*. However, popular Hawaiian wrestler Konishiki outweighs him by more than a hundred pounds *(below)*.

Hazing, intended to instill fighting spirit, is an accepted fact of *beya* life.

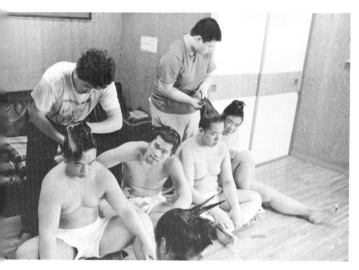

Wrestlers have their hair attended to (*above*) and enjoy the one-pot meal called *chanko-nabe* (*below*).

Tokyo tournaments are held in the new Kokugikan, which opened in 1985.

By the time the higher-ranked wrestlers are ready to meet, the 13,000-seat stadium is filled to capacity.

The ring-entering ceremony of the top-ranked wrestlers is an impressive spectacle. The *rikishi* mount the ring dressed in their *kesho-mawashi (facing page)*. Note the basket of salt and water bucket.

As part of the ring-entering ceremony, wrestlers raise their hands to show that they carry no weapons *(left)*. The ring-entering ceremony of a grand champion is a more complicated affair *(below)*. His elaborately knotted ceremonial belt may weigh over 30 pounds *(lower left)*.

As the announcer calls out their names, the wrestlers mount the *dohyo*, the sumo ring.

Two wrestlers perform *shiko*. This raising and stamping of the feet is intended both as a loosening up exercise and a symbolic exorcism of demons.

Salt throwing is intended to purify the ring *(right)*. Wrestlers squat and try to stare each other down, part of the pre-bout psychological warfare called *shikiri-naoshi (below)*. The staring continues as the *rikishi* stand *(below right)*.

Rikishi lunge toward each other with surprising speed in the initial charge. Open-handed striking, called *tsuppari*, is a technique favored by many wrestlers as a means of keeping opponents off balance *(below left)*. An inside grip on the belt with the right hand will help the *rikishi* on the left to turn and move his rival *(below)*.

After being pushed to the edge of the ring, the *rikishi* on the left is about to fall victim to one of the many kinds of *nage*, or arm throw.

in 1957; and, finally, a *basho* in Nagoya was added in 1958. Today, the annual sumo schedule starts with the Hatsu Basho, or "First Tournament," held in January in Tokyo. The Haru Basho, or "Spring Tournament," is held in Osaka in March, after which Tokyo is again host, for the Natsu Basho, or "Summer Tournament," held in May. The Nagoya Basho is held in July, followed by the Aki Basho, or "Fall Tournament," in Tokyo in September. The Kyushu Basho, held in November, is the last tournament of the year. One can gather two facts from this schedule: that Tokyo is still very much the center of the sumo world, and that, with important bouts on ninety days of the year, *rikishi* must be a very hardy lot indeed.

Common venues for sumo in early Edo days were the Eko-in Temple in Ryogoku and Asakusa Kuramae Hachiman Shrine, both located in the old entertainment quarters of the city, areas still associated with the sport. The largest of the outdoor arenas could hold more than 3,000 people, a sizable number but too small to satisfy the growing legions of fans. Sumo's popularity continued to increase until finally, in 1909, the first Kokugikan, with a seating capacity of 13,000, was built in Ryogoku. Kokugikan literally means "national-sport hall," that is, a stadium for the national sport—sumo—and the naming of the new hall marked the first time such a claim for the sport had been publicly made. The Kokugikan burned to the ground in 1917, was rebuilt, then destroyed again in 1923 during the Great Kanto Earthquake. It was rebuilt again, only to be severely damaged in wartime air raids. For most of the Occupation the stadium was unavailable for sumo, having been renamed Memorial Hall and used, in part, as an ice-skating rink for American soldiers.

However, sumo thrived, again in outdoor venues, and in 1950 construction of a new Kokugikan was begun at Kuramae. Tournaments were held there even before the building was completed. The Kuramae Kokugikan served as the home of sumo until 1985, when the new Ryogoku Kokugikan was opened. Seating over 11,000 and built at a cost of sixty million dollars, the spacious new stadium also houses a sumo training school, clinic, sumo museum, and the offices of the Japan Sumo Association.

That Japan is expensive is a common complaint these days, but for the real sumo fan a day at the new Kokugikan is a bargain. Holding the cheapest ticket (as of this writing, ¥1,200—less than ten dollars), the sumo aficionado can settle into a seat around half past nine in the morning and watch the action until just before six in the evening. This price is for seats in the last, unreserved row, however, and the number of tickets is limited; to be assured of getting one, it is best to get to the stadium early in the day (you can buy a ticket even if you do not enter at that time). It is also a common practice, among both Japanese and foreign fans, to sit in someone else's better, more expensive seat until he or she arrives (this is being reported, not recommended). And, of course, there are more expensive ways to go; a party of four in a fairly good box (if one can be had) will typically spend $150 apiece for the day, with food and drinks.

Aside from the competition, a day at sumo can be quite interesting, for it has its own emotional rhythm; one unconsciously absorbs the feeling of gradually building excitement and suspense. The bouts are held in order of rank, with the junior *rikishi* fighting early in the day, those in one division followed by those of the next higher. There is a casualness about the morning's proceedings—on the part of the spectators, not the wrestlers, of course. Most of the seats are empty, and there is a lot of talking and walking around. Throughout the early afternoon, the seats continue to fill; more attention is paid to the bouts, and the background noise level rises, occasionally to be punctuated by shouts of encouragement to a favored wrestler. Beer, saké, and *o-bento* (Japanese box lunches) appear; the crowd eats, drinks, and becomes a little merrier.

The first of the afternoon's many climaxes occurs with the *dohyo-iri*, or "ring-entering ceremony" of the *juryo* division *rikishi*, around three o'clock. We will look at this ceremony in more detail in the next chapter; here, let us say that it is quite spectacular and commands, for the first time in the day, the rapt attention of the entire audience. More important, it signals the beginning of the *sekitori* bouts, competition between wrestlers in the top two divisions. Also around this time television coverage begins. The cameras require bright lights, and when these come on the crowd for some reason gets livelier and noisier. Perhaps we of the TV generation feel that video coverage brings with it the sanction of importance.

60 • CHAPTER 5

Finally, the wrestlers of the top division (except for the grand champions) arrive and perform their *dohyo-iri*, followed by the *yokozuna* and theirs. This heralds the beginning of the *makunouchi* bouts, which will culminate in those of the grand champions. By this time the atmosphere is charged—the slightest gesture on the *dohyo* brings a reaction from the crowd, and a skillful win brings thunderous applause. But before getting into the actual competition, let us examine briefly some of the tradition informing what spectators see happening before them.

CHAPTER 6

Pageantry, Ritual, and Symbol

Go to a Japanese wedding, attend any traditional musical or theatrical performance, or join in one of the thousands of local festivals held throughout the year, and you will likely sense the Japanese love of pageantry, ritual, and symbol. Not only are these important in religious practice, where one would normally expect to find them, but they seem to permeate business, entertainment, and sport. Sumo is no exception. With its ties to the Shinto religion and its early function as imperial entertainment, one would expect to find it filled with colorful pageantry, ritual gestures, and symbolic trappings. And one is not disappointed.

Ritual and pageantry are at no time more evident than during the *dohyo-iri*, the ring-entering ceremony performed by the top two divisions of wrestlers, the *juryo* and *makunouchi*. The two "sides," east and west, perform their ceremonies separately. Preceded by a referee, the *rikishi* march single file into the arena in order of rank, lowest first, dressed in their colorful *kesho-mawashi*. These are beautiful, elaborately embroidered aprons, usually donated by a wrestler's *koenkai* (patron organization or fan club), and costing from eight thousand dollars up. Their sumptuousness reflects the custom of an earlier era, when *rikishi* were patronized by great lords known as *daimyo*, who used the aprons as a means to display their wealth. Popular wrestlers may have one for each day of the tournament.

As their names are called out by an announcer, the *rikishi* mount the *dohyo* and form a circle within it, facing outward toward the audience. After the last has arrived, the wrestlers turn inward to face each other and perform a ritual that includes clapping, raising the arms into the air, and hoisting the *kesho-mawashi* an inch or two. Each of these movements has significance: the clapping announces to the gods that someone pure is asking for their attention and favor, while the other gestures indicate that no weapons are being carried or concealed. The *rikishi* then depart as they entered. This ceremony is performed four times, by the east and west sides of both top divisions, each day of the tournament.

The ring-entering ceremony for *yokozuna* is, as one would expect, somewhat more elaborate. Led into the arena by the chief referee, a grand champion is also preceded by an attendant called a *tsuyu-harai*, literally "dew-sweeper," and followed by his *tachi-mochi*, the bearer of his long, curved sword. These positions are filled by *maegashira*-ranked wrestlers from the *yokozuna's* stable (or another stable, if wrestlers of sufficiently high rank are not available). Over his *kesho-mawashi*, the grand champion wears his *tsuna*, a thick, white rope that is the emblem of his rank. From it are hung *gohei*, zigzag white paper strips that serve as symbolic offerings to the gods. Both of these religious motifs can be seen decorating Shinto shrines. The *sagari*, the thin band hung with starched silk threads worn by all wrestlers, also reflects a motif of Shinto. The number of threads is usually thirteen, but may be from eleven to nineteen; however, it is always odd, in ancient Oriental number theory symbolic of the male and strength.

On the *dohyo*, the grand champion runs through a complex series of gestures while his attendants squat on either side. In addition to raising the arms and clapping, the ritual of the *yokozuna* includes several *shiko*—the hoisting of a leg high into the air before slamming it to the ground. This gesture, intended to frighten away malignant spirits, is also said to demonstrate the grand champion's intention to crush all opponents.

There are actually two traditional styles of *dohyo-iri*, named after the Edo-period *yokozuna* who supposedly performed them brilliantly: the *unryu* and the *shiranui*. The former was handed down from Unryu Hisakichi (1823–91), the tenth *yokozuna*; the latter was favored by Shiranui Koemon (1825–79), the eleventh. The *unryu* is often described as being defensive, while the *shiranui* is said to be more aggressive. In fact, the two differ only slightly, in the hand movements following the first *shiko*.

The *dohyo* itself is constructed of a special dirt called *rakida*, obtained from Tokyo's neighboring Chiba

Prefecture. The *dohyo* is two feet high and eighteen feet square at the base, and its surface is covered with a thin layer of sand. Embedded in it are straw bales called *tawara*, forming a circle fifteen feet in diameter. (The word *dohyo* is actually a compound of *do*, a variant pronunciation of the character for *tsuchi*, meaning earth, and *hyo*, a variant of *tawara*.) The round and square motifs symbolize heaven and earth. Two of the bales making up the circle are set slightly outside the others. In days of outdoor sumo, this feature allowed rainwater to drain from the ring.

A wooden roof of a design associated with Shinto shrines covers the ring. From its corners are hung four large tassels, signifying the cardinal directions and the seasons of the year: a green tassel to the east, for spring; a red tassel to the south, for summer; a white tassel to the west, for autumn; and a black tassel to the north, for winter. The alignment of the directions, colors, and seasons again reflects ancient Chinese cosmological theory. Until 1952, the roof over the *dohyo* was supported by four large colored poles; these interfered with the view—especially after TV coverage began—and were removed. This roof is now suspended from the stadium roof by means of cables, and the symbolic meanings of the colored poles are now conveyed by the tassels.

The *dohyo* is sacred, and is consecrated in a purification ceremony, the *dohyo-matsuri*, that takes place before the tournament begins. In this ceremony, three white-garbed referees (who for rituals associated with sumo function as Shinto priests) invoke the blessings of the gods on the coming event. The ring is then consecrated by burying symbols of good luck—nuts, seaweed, and dried squid—in an earthenware pot in the center of the ring. An offering of salt and saké, their whiteness and clarity symbolizing purity, is then made.

Once the ring has been purified, no one may stand on it except wrestlers and others with business there—no one in shoes, of course, and absolutely no women. Each day the ring is cleaned, before and after the bouts, according to prescribed Shinto ritual. The spilling of blood during a bout is cause for great concern; if such a defilement should occur, the offending area is scraped clean, brushed, and inspected with great seriousness before the bouts are allowed to proceed.

The *rikishi* themselves take great care to enter the ring in as clean and pure a state as possible. To this end you will see them wipe the sweat from their brows and underarms just before a bout begins. Even before mounting the *dohyo*, they rinse their mouths with water, using a ladle offered to them either by the winner of the previous bout, or, if their side has lost, its representative in the next bout. Once on the *dohyo*, the throwing of salt, again for purification, forms an important part of the pre-bout posturing, the subject of the next chapter. According to the Sumo Association, more than 100 pounds of salt a day are flung into the ring.

CHAPTER 7

Psychological Warfare

A *rikishi's* weapons are of three types. The first are physical—the strength and speed developed through training. The second are technical—the skills and techniques acquired through experience. The third, but by no means least important, are psychological. Since a sumo bout really begins as a psychological confrontation, this latter merits some discussion. It is also, at least to Westerners, one of the more unusual aspects of the sport.

Before each bout, the names of the participants are called out by a *yobidashi*, or announcer. Dressed in kimono and traditional workman's leggings, he mounts the *dohyo* and slowly unfolds a white fan. Facing east and west in turn, he extends his fan and calls out the name of the *rikishi* representing each side in a quavering theatrical voice. As previously mentioned, the east and west division no longer has any basis in fact, but is maintained as an organizing device for tournament bouts and listings. Pairings are announced a day in advance throughout the tournament and cannot be changed. If a wrestler must drop out after the announcement of the pairings, the bout counts as a loss.

The *yobidashi* descends from the *dohyo* as the two combatants mount it from the east and west. As they begin their warming up exercises, their names are announced once more, this time by the referee, called a *gyoji*, in a shout that begins powerfully but then fades in volume. If the bout is between top-division wrestlers, other *yobidashi*, carrying pennants suspended from long poles, may mount the *dohyo* and parade around it. The flags represent additional prize money offered by sponsors to the winner of the bout; the pennants are advertisements for the sponsors—Tokyo Disneyland, for example. Before a particularly crucial bout, or one between arch rivals, a dozen or so pennants may appear, each worth about $320. (Actually, only about half the money goes directly to the winner; the rest goes to funds set up to take care of the *rikishi's* taxes and retirement, and to the Sumo Association, for "expenses.")

Following an initial flexing of muscles and stamping of feet at the edge of the ring, the rivals go to opposite corners and rinse their mouths with a ladle of water provided by a fellow wrestler. After wiping their lips with a piece of special white paper (*chikara-gami*, or "paper of strength"), they pick up a handful of salt and heave it over the *dohyo*. Both of these gestures are acts of ritual purification that have been performed before sumo bouts for more than three centuries.

The *rikishi* now squat near the center of the ring and face each other from a respectful distance. They fix each other with piercing stares, pound the *dohyo*, stand, slap themselves, and generally try to scare the hell out of each other. This ritual, known as the *shikiri-naoshi*, is often unimpressive to those whose definition of competition encompasses only its physical dimension. For most Western fans of TV sports, the *shikiri-naoshi* seems a good time for a commercial break. But for the true aficionado, this outrageous posturing is the heart of sumo, and veteran watchers even claim to be able to pick a winner on the basis of a *rikishi's* performance.

It might seem incredible that a three-hundred-pound professional wrestler could ever be psyched out. But these *rikishi* fight each other often and each is well aware of his opponent's relative skills, strengths and weaknesses, and even his fears and aspirations. To stare a rival straight in the eye takes concentration and will, and it is readily apparent if one is "off"—physically or psychologically.

Four minutes are allotted for the *shikiri-naoshi* of *makunouchi* wrestlers; three minutes for *rikishi* in the *juryo* division. Those in the lower divisions have time for only a perfunctory glare or gesture or none at all. During the *sekitori's* performance, however, the squatting, standing, staring, and salt throwing is repeated several times. The full allotted time does not have to be used; whenever the *rikishi* feel ready, they can leap from the crouching position and clash, in a coordinated move called *tachi-ai*. If they continue their *shikiri-naoshi*, a judge will eventually call time and signal the *yobidashi* and referee to get the bout started. After wiping their faces and armpits, the *rikishi* crouch and face each other for the last time; the referee holds his fan flat against his chest to signal that the bout must begin. There is no precise signal for the start of the *tachi-ai*—the charge is naturally and spontaneously synchronized. There is, however, an unwritten rule that the hands must touch the ground before the forward lunge.

Rikishi are huge men but the speed of their forward lunge in the *tachi-ai* can be breathtaking, and often results in a resounding thwack when their two bodies or heads meet. Some *rikishi* prefer to grab directly for their opponent's belt; a good grip on the *mawashi* is considered a key to victory. Other wrestlers, however, prefer to push and slap their opponents backward, keeping them continually off balance, and still others may sidestep their opponent's initial charge. A wide range of offensive and defensive techniques are employed (the subject of chapter eight) but the rules of sumo are simple and straightforward. The loser is the first *rikishi* to leave the ring or to touch the ground with any part of his body, other than the feet, of course. There are also some proscribed tactics: striking with a closed fist, poking the eyes, pulling the hair, kicking the stomach, choking, and grabbing any part of the *mawashi* that covers the genital area.

It is the *gyoji's* responsibility to keep the action going. As soon as the *tachi-ai* commences, he begins to sidestep quickly around the *rikishi*, yelling out, *"Nokotta, nokotta!"* meaning roughly "You're still in there!" Occasionally, an extended period of grappling and shoving results in no advantage gained by either side; the *rikishi* stand in the center of the ring locked in each other's grip. Although they appear drained and immobile, a close look shows an occasional flexing of the muscles as they test each other's capacity to resist a pull or shove. At such times the referee yells out *"Yoi! Hakkeyoi!"* or "Get a move on!" On rare occasions the match is treated as a temporary stalemate; the wrestlers retire to their respective dressing rooms and return to meet each other again after a rest lasting two bouts. There are no ties in sumo; sooner or later, someone goes down or out.

The *gyoji* decides the winner or loser of a bout and no *rikishi* will question his decision (although ringside judges can and do, as will be seen in chapter ten). When the winner of a bout has been decided, the vanquished party makes a curt bow to his opponent and retires. There is little show of emotion on the part of either winner or loser; to gloat or sulk is considered bad form. The *gyoji* raises his fan and announces the name of the victor. He then squats and presents the envelopes containing the prizes for the victory on the flat side of his fan. The winning *rikishi* makes three deft chops in the air with his hand—signifying thanks to heaven, earth, and man—before picking up the envelopes. Before leaving the auditorium, he offers a ladle of water—*chikara-mizu*—the "water of strength"—to the next wrestler on his side.

In former days of outdoor sumo, fans would signal their approval of a bout by throwing things into the ring—often money, fruit, or food for the winner. That practice was eliminated as being unseemly, although after the final bout of the day, particularly if it has been an exciting one, you may see appreciative fans throw their cushions into the *dohyo*. This mild display of exuberance is about as rowdy as the audience gets, surprising considering the quantities of beer and saké consumed. Sumo fans are for the most part well-dressed and well-mannered, although they are enthusiastic and quite vocal. Favored wrestlers are encouraged with shouts of "*Ganbare!*" or "Go for it!"; those less well-liked may hear "*Makeru-zo!*"—"You're going to lose!"

Following the last bout, a lower-ranked *rikishi* performs an interesting ceremony involving the twirling of a long bow. Called the *yumitori-shiki*, this ritual is said to date from the Heian era, when the tournament winner was presented with a long bow as a symbol of his victory. This brings the tournament day officially to a close. But before leaving the Kokugikan, let's examine more carefully some of the favored techniques used by the *rikishi* to win.

CHAPTER 8

Sumo Techniques

By the end of the preliminary posturing called *shikiri-naoshi*, the *rikishi* has—or should have—made up his mind how he will handle the imminent onrush of his rival.

Some wrestlers like to go straight for the belt, securing a grip on the *mawashi* that will give them control. Others invariably prefer not to do so. They like to slap an opponent toward the edge of the ring, a technique called *tsuppari*, and then, when their man is off-balance, push him out. Both Konishiki and Hokutoumi excel at this type of sumo, and are able to deliver thrusts to an opponent's upper chest, throat, and face sufficiently powerful to force him out without ever getting a hold on the body or belt. A victory by this method is called *tsuki-dashi* (literally, "thrust out") if the loser is pushed outside the ring; *tsuki-taoshi* ("thrust down") if he goes down inside the ring. (These should not be confused with *oshi-dashi*, or "push out," the most common winning technique, and *oshi-taoshi*, or "push down." With these two techniques, more continuous contact is maintained.) *Tsuppari* is a valuable weapon in wrestler's armory. It saves strength—an important consideration in a fifteen-day tournament—and it reduces the likelihood of leg injuries, a constant problem of the bigger *rikishi*.

If a *rikishi* senses that his opponent is overanxious to launch into his *tachi-ai*, he may simply sidestep the charge, turn and push his off-balance opponent down with a swift and hard smack on the back. This technique, called *hataki-komi*, has caught many a fan napping and caused him or her to miss the bout. Kotogaume and Takanofuji both commonly employ this technique, although all *rikishi* use it at one time or another.

Although a good burst of *tsuppari* is an exciting way to get a bout started, most dyed-in-the-wool fans prefer to watch the grappling techniques of sumo. With several noted exceptions, such as the behemoth Konishiki mentioned above, it is the heavier wrestlers who naturally prefer to take the fullest advantage of their weight by coming to grips with their opponents as quickly as possible. In the clinch, the best advantage is obtained by having a grip on the opponent's belt with the hand inside his. If this is done with the left hand, it is called *hidari-yotsu*; if it is done with the right hand, it is called *migi-yotsu*. Having both hands on an opponent's belt and inside his arms is a position called *moro-zashi*. A wrestler will try to keep an opponent from getting a grip on his belt by squirming about and keeping the lower part of the body at a safe distance.

There are numerous holds and throws in sumo, from which several lists of orthodox winning techniques have been compiled. Illustrated here are the most common of these techniques; the wrestler wearing the black belt will be the winner.

Maki-otoshi

Uwate-nage Hatakikomi Yorikiri Ashi-tori

Nimaigeri Shitate-dashinage Uttchari Shitate-yagura

Sotogake Uchigake Nodowa-zeme Kubi-nage

Uwate-dashinage

Watashikomi

Kote-nage

Taller wrestlers are naturally more adept at these maneuvers, an advantage offset by their higher centers of gravity.

Once a grip on the belt is secured, a tactic favored by the bigger men is to use their weight advantage to gradually edge their opponents toward the rim of the *dohyo* and gently march them out. Known as *yori-kiri*, this is a very common winning technique. A more exciting variant is *yori-taoshi*, in which the vanquished, sometimes locked tightly in the grip of the victor, goes hurtling out of the ring and crashes to the ground.

Kirishima is one of several wrestlers fond of *tsuri-dashi* (lift out). These *rikishi* like to grasp an opponent's *mawashi* firmly with both hands, push or pull him around till he's off-balance and finally hoist him high in the air and out of the ring, against some rivals a truly Herculean feat. Then there's the spectacular *utchari*. This occurs when a *rikishi*, on the point of being toppled out, digs in at the edge of the ring, hoists his rival up over his stomach and, with a quick turn, flings him out. This is an emergency technique that might be used by any wrestler, although Daitetsu is somewhat of a specialist in it.

Other tactics are aimed at dumping a man inside the ring. Some wrestlers are adept at using their legs to trip an opponent. One such technique is called *uchi-gake* (inside leg trip); timing his move carefully, a wrestler will suddenly thrust a leg through his rival's legs and upset him with a neat trip. Others favor the *soto-gake*, in which a leg is wound outside the opponent's—with the same result.

The beautiful *uwate-nage* is an arm throw by which lighter men, such as Chiyonofuji and Sakahoko, often overthrow much heavier opponents. It might be translated as "upper-hand throw," the "upper" referring to the hand that is outside the other man's arm; the throw is executed with this outside hand, using the hips as a fulcrum over which to pull and thrust down the victim. The "opposite" of this maneuver is the *shitate-nage*, or "under-hand throw," in which the throw is executed using the power of the inside hand. Both Onokuni and Hananoumi make frequent use of this throw. More often than not a lot of maneuvering takes place and several fruitless attempts are made at a throw before an opponent is finally caught off-balance and flung down.

There are several traditional lists specifying forty-eight orthodox winning techniques, or *kimari-te*, although the Sumo Association today officially recognizes seventy, many of them simply minor variations. To describe them all would require a volume in itself, but a study of the line drawings on pages 74–75 will allow fans to recognize those most commonly used.

A tournament is won by the top-division *rikishi* who has racked up the best won-lost record over the fifteen days of competition. The victory is called a *yusho*, and, if the *rikishi's* record is unblemished by a single loss, it is called a *zensho-yusho*. In former days, the *yusho* would go to the senior man in case of tying records; now a play-off bout is held instead. If two wrestlers finish up on the last day with identical winning records, they will meet in an extra bout, after the closing ceremony. On occasion, this has resulted in two top *rikishi* fighting twice in a row on the last day, quite an exciting windup for a tournament.

Each division of sumo has a tournament winner, but the focus is naturally on the winner of the top, *makunouchi*, division. That lucky *rikishi* receives an incredible variety and quantity of prizes and trophies, in a ceremony held after the last bout on the last day. Foremost among the spoils is the Emperor's Cup and a banner attesting to his victory given by the Sumo Association. He is also given a number of practical prizes—large quantities of dried mushrooms, whiskey, rice, and other goods.

As exciting as they are, tournaments are not necessarily the best place to watch *rikishi* in action. A much better, and often cheaper, seat can usually be obtained for one of the provincial, one-day exhibitions, held in various locations between the six Grand Tournaments. Called *jungyo*, provincial touring is undertaken to promote sumo in areas where it is not normally seen. The regions are fixed, but the schedule varies; it can be obtained by calling or writing (in Japanese) the Japan Sumo Association (the address and telephone number are listed on page 119) just prior to the end of each tournament.

CHAPTER 9

The Grand Champions

Around eleven hundred years ago, the story goes, there lived in Omi Province an incredibly powerful wrestler by the name of Hajikami. Invited to join in a tournament of ritual sumo held at a Shinto shrine, he easily overpowered all the other contenders—so easily, in fact, that the referee decided a handicap was necessary to restore fairness to the proceedings. Removing the *shimenawa*, the sacred rope, from the front of the shrine, the referee wound it around Hajikami's waist, declaring that any wrestler who could even put his hands on it would be judged the winner. But such was Hajikami's strength and skill that no one could even get close.

This is one of several stories that purport to account for how the great champions of sumo came to be called *yokozuna*, literally "horizontal rope"; the great white hawser that is the mark of their rank is called a *tsuna* (pronounced *zuna* in this combination). Official use of the term, however, can be said to date from only 1789, when one Yoshida Oikaze, in a bid to strengthen his control of the sumo world, gained legal authority to grant a document called the *menkyo*, a kind of "yokozuna license." Still, the term was only one of several used to designate the top wrestlers, and did not appear on a *banzuke* until about a hundred years later. Finally, in 1909 the Japan Sumo Association issued a proclamation declaring *yokozuna* the highest rank in sumo. Their number is not fixed. As of this writing there are three, but at times in the past there have been as many as five and as few as none.

Ironically, Hajikami was never proclaimed a grand champion. The honor of being the first was reserved for another sumo great, Akashi Shiganosuke, a figure about whom there is actually no precise record available and who is probably fictional. In the early part of the seventeenth century, it is said, a great tournament was held at the imperial court in Kyoto. Akashi, the son of a samurai, defeated Nio Nidaya of Nagasaki to win the tourney and become the first official *yokozuna* in the history of sumo. He reputedly stood over eight feet tall and weighed over four hundred pounds, but the figures are not official, and he has no doubt grown in stature with every passing generation. We are on much firmer ground when we come to Tanikaze Kajinosuke, the fourth grand champion and possibly the greatest of them all. He was born in 1750, the son of a poor farmer from Japan's northern Tohoku region. In the *makunouchi* division, including seven years as *yokozuna*, Tanikaze piled up an amazing record of 258 wins and 14 losses. That gives him an average of .948. His achievement of going through sixty-three consecutive bouts without a defeat has been bettered only by Futabayama's sixty-nine. In contrast to some of his legendary predecessors, Tanikaze was a mere six feet two inches in height, and his 350 pounds put him in about the same class physically as the modern Kirinishiki. He finally succumbed, not to an opponent in the ring but to an attack of influenza, and died in 1795 at the age of forty-five. A Japanese saying has it that "There was never the equal of Tanikaze, before or since."

Hitachiyama, the nineteenth *yokozuna*, was another all-time great. After attaining *makunouchi* rank, he lost only eight times in eighteen tournaments, over a period of nine years. An amazing wrestler, he might also be considered the prototype of the modern sumo man, since he was the first *rikishi* ever to go abroad. In 1907 he visited the United States, where he was presented to Teddy Roosevelt. Visitors to the Sumo Museum at Kokugikan may see the top hat and walking stick that Hitachiyama sported when he went to the States. Naturally, he took his ceremonial apron with him to show it off. Hitachiyama's *kesho-mawashi* was rather special. It was studded with diamonds and worth millions.

While glancing over the colorful ranks of past grand champions, we shouldn't overlook mighty Kitanoumi, who in 1974, at the age of twenty-one years and two months, became the youngest grand champion ever.

The opposite sort of record was established by the twelfth *yokozuna*, Jinmaku, in the mid-nineteenth century. He was thirty-nine when he attained the rank of grand champion, an age at which most *rikishi* have long since retired.

Over the course of his career, Kitanoumi chalked up a total of 804 wins, surpassing the record of 746 wins set by the still living but already legendary Taiho. There is also some possibility that Taiho's record of thirty-two *yusho* may be bested by the current grand champion Chiyonofuji, who in 1988 broke the former *yokozuna's* record of forty-five consecutive bout victories, going on to win fifty-three in a row. This put Chiyonofuji in second place behind Futabayama for the record of most consecutive wins in modern sumo.

There is a growing consensus among sumo fans that Chiyonofuji will be one of tomorrow's legends; he must certainly be considered the most powerful wrestler of the past decade. At six feet even and wrestling at about 270 pounds, he is one of the lighter men of sumo, proof, were any needed, that strength, speed, and technique will always win out over bulk alone.

Nicknamed "the Wolf" for his piercing lupine glare during the *shikiri-naoshi* and his ferocity when cornered, Chiyonofuji's career was a little slow to get started but is having a spectacular windup, if indeed it is even close to being over. Born in 1955, he attained the rank of *yokozuna* when he was twenty-six. As he approached thirty, an age at which most *rikishi* are planning their retirements, he simply got better, racking up one tournament victory after another and winning more *yusho* after thirty than has any *rikishi* this century. As of early 1989, Chiyonofuji had racked up a remarkable twenty-five tournament wins.

A hot topic among sumo fans is how long Chiyonofuji will or can continue to dominate sumo. Chiyonofuji himself says that he would like to stay in the sport until he is thirty-six or so, which would make it possible for him to break Taiho's all-time record of thirty-two *yusho*. What this means for fans and potential fans of sumo is simply this: Now is a good time to be watching because, legends notwithstanding, one of the sports all-time greats can be seen in action.

The other two *yokozuna* currently wrestling are Hokutoumi and Onokuni. A rule of sumo is that *rikishi* from the same stable do not wrestle each other unless, on the final day, it is necessary to determine the tournament winner. This has kept Hokutoumi, a stablemate of Chiyonofuji at Kokonoe Beya, somewhat out of the limelight. Moreover, a back injury resulted in an extended layoff after he was promoted to the top spot in 1987. However, with his solid victory in the first basho of 1989, he is expected to be a dependably strong grand champion, and since he is eight years younger than Chiyonofuji, he will likely be around a lot longer. A great technician possessing a wide variety of sumo skills, Hokutoumi is a scrappy and tenacious wrestler. For this reason, as well as for his short but solid stature (five feet eleven inches and 318 pounds), he is often referred to as "the Bulldog."

At six feet two inches and nearly 450 pounds, Onokuni, the third of the *yokozuna* trio presently fighting, is the largest Japanese-born wrestler ever, surpassing in bulk even the legendary champions of past ages. Popularly known as "the Panda," for obvious reasons, Onokuni lacks speed; had he been blessed with more, he might have been one of the greatest wrestlers ever. Still, Onokuni is a solid wrestler in the classic mold, using his weight to power out opponents through *yori-kiri* and *oshi-dashi*. A former judo champion, he is also good at grabbing the belt. One year older than Hokutoumi, Onokuni should have several good years left in sumo.

Who gains the rank of *yokozuna* is largely determined by a special Yokozuna Review Committee (sometimes translated Yokozuna Promotion Council). This advisory body, made up of distinguished men from outside the sport, makes recommendations to the Japan Sumo Association, which invariably accepts them. Unlike wrestlers in the lower ranks, *yokozuna* cannot be demoted. Appointing them must consequently be done with great care and such a promotion comes with a great deal of responsibility; a *yokozuna* must continually maintain a record worthy of the title, or else retire. According to the rules, this ultimate advancement is only accorded *ozeki* who have won two consecutive tournaments. As this is a nearly impossible achievement, however (although it has been done), a provision allows for "equivalent success" as evidence of a wrestler's merit.

When the advancement is made official, the new *yokozuna's* stablemates prepare his first *tsuna* and he is instructed in the ceremony of the *dohyo-iri* for his rank.

The Grand Champions · 85

A special ritual is conducted at Tokyo's Meiji Shrine, where the *tsuna* is blessed and the wrestler receives the documents attesting to his promotion. The pinnacle of success in the sumo world has at last been attained. When one reflects on the fact that there are usually about 800 active wrestlers vying for a position that only three or four can hold, one can see that it is a signal honor, indeed.

CHAPTER 10

Referees and Judges

The *gyoji*, or referee, in sumo takes a role of far greater importance than does his counterpart in Western sports. He is, in fact, a leading player in the theater of sumo, without whom the show literally could not go on.

In previous chapters we looked at some of the *gyoji's* varied and important duties. He oversees the action in the ring—starting the bouts and keeping them going, declaring the winner, and awarding the prizes. And he has important ceremonial functions—consecrating the ring and keeping it pure, and heading the retinue of the grand champions during their *dohyo-iri*.

Of course, one man is not responsible for all these tasks. There are many referees, arrayed in a hierarchy identical to that of the *rikishi*. The rank of a referee can be roughly determined by his costume and fan: the more sumptuous, the higher the rank. The *gyoji's* specific rank can be determined from the color of his trimmings—the tassel hanging from his fan and the braid and rosettes at the collar and cuffs of his heavy silk kimono. Those of the *tate-gyoji*, or head referee, are purple, while his assistant is trimmed in purple and white. Referees at the *sanyaku* level (the three ranks below grand champion), wear bright red, while other *makunouchi*-level *gyoji* are adorned with red and white. *Juryo*-level referees wear green-and-white tassels and trim, while those below *juryo* may wear either green or black.

Referees begin training in their specialty at around age fifteen or sixteen. It is an attractive job and successful candidates often come from families closely associated with sumo. Once selected, all referees take the name of either Shikimori or Kimura, the two families that dominated the occupation during the Edo period. Referees from the two families can be distinguished by the slightly different manner with which they grip the fan when announcing the wrestlers for a bout; those who are Shikimori-affiliated turn their thumb and fingers upward, while Kimura-affiliated referees turn theirs downward.

Trainees begin refereeing the bouts of the lowest-ranked *rikishi*, and gradually work their way through the referee hierarchy as their technique and judgment improve. Promotion does not come quickly or automatically, however. Advancement depends upon seniority and, as the total number of positions is fixed, the pace can be excruciatingly slow. Moreover, promotion can be delayed through the acquisition of excessive demerits during the course of a tournament, the penalty for making an erroneous judgment of a bout's victor.

Given the simplicity of the criteria for besting an opponent—forcing him down or out—it might seem that a bad call would be out of the question. But quite often two wrestlers hit the ground nearly simultaneously; it takes keen attention and the skill (or good fortune) to be properly positioned to catch the errant elbow or knee that may have brushed the sand first.

To ensure that a fair call is made each time, a panel of five judges watches every bout. Called *shimpan*, they are seated at the center of each side of the *dohyo*, with an extra judge, responsible for keeping time, on one side. All are well-known, retired wrestlers, elders in the Sumo Association, and are easily spotted due to their size and their formal black attire. Since they outnumber the *gyoji* and are better positioned to witness the crucial determining moment of the bout, judges will occasionally dispute the referee's decision about the winner. When this occurs, the judges climb up on the *dohyo* and hold a brief conference known as *mono-ii*, literally, "talking about matters." Three possible courses of action can result from such a conference: to affirm the *gyoji's* decision, to reverse the decision, or to hold a rematch. Called *tori-naoshi*, rematches take place immediately and are always a big hit with the fans, who like nothing better than a close match.

To help maintain their concentration, judges perform their duties in shifts, with four shifts being rotated throughout the day. Judges also change their seating positions from shift to shift, to gain the experience of

The referee continually tries to keep in a good position to view the action, but there are many tough calls *(above)*. A black-robed judge, or *shimpan*, keeps a wary eye on the proceedings *(below)*. It is plain to see he is a former *rikishi*.

When a call is disputed, the five ringside judges gather in *mono ii*, to "talk about things."

The *dohyo* is sacred ground; sweepers work periodically to keep its surface clean and smooth.

Getting both hands on an opponent's belt, called *moro-zashi*, gives a *rikishi* commanding control *(left)*. His unfortunate rival is soon flipped up, over, and out of the *dohyo* *(below)*.

The happy winner of a grand tournament, Hokutoumi accepts the Emperor's Cup *(right)*. Chiyonofuji instructs Hokutoumi, newly promoted to grand champion, in the ring-entering ceremony for his rank *(below)*.

The last bout of each tournament day is followed by a bow-twirling ceremony. The day's sumo action has come to an end.

viewing the action from different vantage points. During shift changes, the ring is carefully wetted down and swept, especially on top of and just outside the straw bales, so that the evidence of a hand or foot outside the ring will be clearly visible.

All of these measures are taken to ensure scrupulous fairness and accuracy in determining bout winners, but even with such precautions the system has not been infallible. Press photographs in the past have proven that even conferences of judges have resulted in erroneous decisions. One particularly notorious incident occurred in March of 1969. A referee's decision that the great *yokozuna* Taiho had just won his forty-sixth consecutive victory was reversed by the judges after a *mono-ii*. Film footage and photos developed later showed that the judges were in error; Taiho had clearly won. However, the decision stood, and Taiho's streak was snapped at forty-five. It was subsequently decided that judges should have access to video replays. Video coverage of tournaments is now monitored in a separate room by two additional judges, who can report their decisions to the *dohyo* via a small earphone worn by the head judge.

Judges have other duties away from the *dohyo*. The two most important of these are the *banzuke-hensei*, the preparation of the list of wrestlers for each tournament, and the *torikumi-hensei*, the choice of pairings for the daily bouts. The first of these tasks is accomplished three days after the end of each tournament. The work must be attended to so quickly because there are usually promotions, often requiring a *rikishi* to make some preparations. A new *juryo* wrestler, for example, will need a silk *mawashi* and an embroidered *kesho-mawashi* for the next tournament. Newly appointed *yokozuna* are particularly busy, as they must have their *tsuna* prepared, master the *dohyo-iri* for their rank, and be formally installed at Meiji Shrine.

The matching of wrestlers for individual bouts is not fixed in advance, but takes place daily throughout tournaments. This has been the cause of carping by some who feel that the pairings should be less manipulated, but the judges have a very sensible purpose in mind—to make the tournament more exciting. Those *rikishi* favored to take the *yusho* will usually not begin to meet each other until the beginning of the second week. By this time there may be three, four, or five *rikishi* with records good enough to be still in contention. If the judges are doing their job well and have a little luck going for them, the tournament winner will not emerge until the last day, and then perhaps only after a thrilling, final, tie-breaking bout between two grand champions.

CHAPTER 11

What's in a Name?

A sumo name, or *shikona*, is a symbol, and, as with all symbols of sumo, it is accorded great respect and never taken lightly. Selection of a proper *shikona* is vital; yet as important as it is to the *rikishi* who bears it, he often has little choice in its selection. He may be allowed some opinion in the matter, but the stablemaster makes the final choice, based on his own expectations for the *rikishi* being named, stable tradition, and custom.

A proper *shikona* links the *rikishi* to something powerful, and the association is a source of strength. The connection may be to an important natural feature sacred to Shinto, or perhaps to a past champion of the same stable. A look at some of the names popular in the sumo world should help to make this clear.

Two of the most common characters found in *rikishi* names are *yama* and *fuji*. The former is the Japanese for "mountain," while the latter is usually written with the characters for Mount Fuji. A mountain, of course, is the perfect natural metaphor for a *rikishi*: broad at the base, majestic in stature, imperturbable and immovable. And a logical choice for a particular mountain would be Japan's tallest—Mount Fuji, symbol of the nation and sacred to Shinto. *Fuji* forms part of the names of wrestlers Chiyonofuji, Asahifuji, and Takanofuji, while *yama* appears in Daijuyama and Koboyama, among others.

Every *rikishi* cannot be a mountain, however. Some must be content with names that include *kawa* (or *gawa*, when it appears in combination) and *umi*, meaning "river" and "sea," respectively. One can see that an ocean is majestic and powerful, but a river is not so obviously awe-inspiring. However, in Eastern tradition, water is considered efficacious in many ways. Taoist texts use water as a symbol of virtuous power: it seeks the lowest level yet benefits all things; it moves slowly, but ultimately overcomes anything in its path. And in Shinto, water is a purifying agent. We have seen how wrestlers rinse their mouths with it before bouts, just as visitors do before entering the precincts of Shinto shrines. *Rikishi* whose names include the Japanese for "river" and "sea" are Wakasegawa and the *yokozuna* Hokutoumi. And there are several other names incorporating water-related words. The *izumi* in Mitoizumi means "spring," for example.

The Japanese word for island, *shima*, forms part of the *shikona* of several wrestlers, including Akinoshima and Kirishima (both place names). Like a mountain, an island is an enduring, immovable natural feature. It is a logical component of names of participants in the traditional sport of an island nation. Indeed, the Japanese are a patriotic, some would say nationalistic, people. It is therefore not surprising that *kuni* and *koku*, variant pronunciations of the character for "country," form part of some wrestlers' names. The name of the current *yokozuna* Onokuni means "Big Country," appropriate for a 450-pound behemoth, while that of Hananokuni means "Country of Flowers." The name taken by the *sekitori* Ryogoku meaning "Two Countries," actually comes from the Ryogoku area of Tokyo, where the national sumo stadium and most of the *beya* are located.

As they do in the West, the dragon and phoenix figure prominently in Oriental mythology. In the East, however, the dragon is not a fire-breathing kidnaper of damsels, but a benevolent creature whose appearance heralds good fortune. Dragons are also closely associated with water; they dwell in rivers and lakes and are credited with bringing life-sustaining rain. The Japanese for dragon is *ryu*, which forms part of the names of *rikishi* Tamaryu, literally "Jewel Dragon," and Dairyu, or "Big Dragon."

The wrestler Ho-o has an interesting name, made up of the characters for the male and female phoenix, a mythical bird said to appear only in times of peace and prosperity. The phoenix of the Orient is quite a splendid bird, supposedly six feet in height with feathers of five colors, symbolizing the five cardinal virtues of Confucianism. The etymology of the characters for phoenix indicates that it is the emperor of birds and, like the Emperor of Japan, it is closely associated with the sun and with *yang*, the powerful, male principle of the universe. Indeed, the symbol of Japan is the rising sun, which can be signified by a character pronounced *asahi*, which forms part of the name Asahifuji, "Sunrise Over Mount Fuji."

The *shikona* of some wrestlers incorporate the character for "brocade," pronounced *nishiki*. This derives from earlier days of sumo when bolts of embroidered silk were given as prizes to winning *rikishi*. Wrestlers with this character in their names are Kirinishiki, or "Victorious Brocade," and Konishiki, meaning "Little Brocade." The latter seems a rather dainty name for someone who weighs more than a quarter of a ton, but it was formerly used by a great *rikishi* from the same stable.

Shikona of former sumo greats are often assigned promising *rikishi*. For example, Chiyonoyama was an outstanding *rikishi* in the 1940s. His name means, literally, "Mountain of a Thousand Generations," or perhaps, "Eternal Mountain." He joined the Dewanoumi stable in 1942 at age sixteen and was promoted to *yokozuna*, the first from Japan's northern island of Hokkaido, in 1951. He retired eight years later after winning six *yusho* and compiling a lifetime record of 366 wins and 149 losses. He subsequently opened a stable under the name of Kokonoe, where he trained the fifty-second grand champion, Kitanofuji, or "Northern Fuji." A decade later he recruited another promising young wrestler from Hokkaido. In honor of his mentors, the new *rikishi* took the name Chiyonofuji, "Eternal Fuji."

A wrestler's *beya* is often evident from his name. Hananoumi, or "Sea of Flowers," Hananokuni, or "Country of Flowers," and Hananofuji, or "Wisteria Blossoms" all are members of the Hanaregoma stable. The word *hana*, you have no doubt surmised, means "flower," and in Japanese carries the same connotation of perfection that its English equivalent does in the West. Several *beya* have proprietary *shikona*. Any *rikishi* whose name begins with Dewa- will belong to the Dewanoumi Beya; any whose name begins with Tatsu- will hail from the Tatsunami Beya. In some cases, every *rikishi* in the *beya* will be given a name associated with it; the *shikona* of every member of the Sadogatake Beya, for example, begins with Koto-.

A wrestler may bear several names over the course of his association with sumo. He may change it in an attempt to improve his luck or to mark some particularly momentous event in his career. Hokutoumi, for example, formerly wrestled under his real name, Hoshi. When he was promoted to *yokozuna*, he assumed his present name, which means "Northern Victorious Sea," reflecting his Hokkaido origins. Upon retirement, most top wrestlers want to become members of the Japan Sumo Association. This entails the assumption of yet another name, since association members are limited to a fixed number of traditional surnames. Thus, Hokutoumi will likely go by at least three different names, a typical number, during the course of his career.

Incidentally, in case you should be introduced to a top-ranked wrestler, not entirely unlikely if you are out on the town in the Ryogoku area, they are addressed with the honorific suffix -*zeki*, as in, for example, Ryogoku-*zeki*. This derives from the term *sekitori*, used to denote wrestlers in the top two divisions. Actually, sumo *rikishi* are generally a friendly and well-behaved crowd, and would likely not object to being addressed with -*san*, the ordinary Japanese suffix for surnames, which can be used for lower-ranked wrestlers.

CHAPTER 12

The Spoils of Victory

As with all other privileges and responsibilities in the world of sumo, monetary compensation is accorded by rank and differs widely between the top and bottom rungs of the sport. Only *rikishi* in the top two classes—*juryo* and *makunouchi*—receive regular salaries. *Yokozuna* now earn $8,200 per month; *ozeki* $6,800; and so on down the line. (Monetary amounts are calculated here at ¥125=US $1.00.) Wrestlers in the lower divisions must be content with an allowance for participation in each tournament, called *basho-teate*, ranging from $720 for *makushita* wrestlers down to $480 for *rikishi* in the *jonokuchi* division.

However, salaries and tournament allowances alone do not give an accurate picture of the rewards of a career in sumo. There are literally dozens of other forms of direct and indirect compensation for the higher-ranking *rikishi*: supplementary allowances for

Tokyo tournaments, travel allowances for provincial tours, and subsidies for the replacement of a grand champion's *tsuna*. There is also a separate form of compensation calculated on the basis of past performance. New *rikishi* are credited with a small amount—three yen—to which is added a half yen for each victory in excess of *kachi-koshi* (a simple majority of wins). When a wrestler attains *sekitori* status he receives every month the total he has accumulated multiplied by 1,500, on top of his basic salary. The base figure is called *hoshokin*, or incentive pay.

There are also prizes: prizes for tournament victories in each class *(yusho)*, prizes for bout victories in the *makunouchi* division *(kensho)*, special prizes for the display of fighting spirit *(kanto-sho)*, technique *(gino-sho)*, and for an outstanding tournament performance *(shukun-sho)*. For each *yusho* and special prize a sum is also added to the wrestler's *hoshokin*.

Then there are gifts from supporters and fan clubs, honorariums for participation in public and private events, fees for the use of a *rikishi's* name and image by commercial sponsors and, when a wrestler's fighting days are over, a large retirement bonus from the Japan Sumo Association. In fact, the total earnings by a successful wrestler over a lifetime can be enormous and are virtually impossible for an outsider to calculate with any degree of accuracy.

But it can be fun to try. Let us take, for example, the reigning superstar of sumo, Chiyonofuji. In addition to his monthly salary of $8,200, he receives a $24,000 bonus for each tournament in which he participates.

He also gets $40,000 for each tournament victory (twenty-five as of early 1989) and $280 *kensho* for each victorious bout. Honorariums range from $8,000 for an appearance at an autograph-signing party to $24,000 for participation in ceremonial sumo at a Shinto shrine. Chiyonofuji's popularity is reflected in the sizable gifts he receives from supporters; after his victory in the 1988 Kyushu Basho, he was reportedly given $160,000 by his ecstatic fans.

The weekly magazine *Shukan Shincho* estimated that Chiyonofuji has received around $6.4 million since attaining the rank of *yokozuna*. And when he finally does retire from the sport, he is scheduled to receive a $560,000 retirement bonus from the Sumo Association, as well as an $800,000 special merit award, plus the proceeds from his retirement ceremony, which should amount to another $800,000. The rewards for those who make it to the very top of this sport are truly great.

And what of life after sumo? As can be readily inferred, the career of the *rikishi* is not an easy one. To be battered and smashed by opponents weighing hundreds of pounds on ninety days of the year (for regular tournaments, not to mention countless practice and exhibition bouts) really takes its toll. The unusual career of Chiyonofuji aside, most *rikishi* begin contemplating retirement as they near their thirties.

To mark the occasion of a *rikishi's* retirement, a special ceremony is held, called a *danpatsu-shiki*, which involves the ritual removal of his topknot. The *rikishi* sits in a chair in the center of the *dohyo*, while the wrestler's patrons, who have made a sizable donation for the privilege of participating, file forward one by one and snip off a few hairs, avoiding the topknot. The snipping is done with gold-plated scissors, held by a referee. The patrons are followed by the *rikishi's* fellow wrestlers and Sumo Association officials. Finally, the stablemaster himself steps forward and cuts off the topknot, which the *rikishi* may keep as a memento of his career in the sport.

A top-ranking wrestler usually stays in sumo even after retirement by becoming an elder in the Japan Sumo Association, a prestigious position that guarantees an income for life. As the number of elders is fixed at 105, however, this option is obviously not open to every *rikishi*. Those aspiring to membership in this elite group must purchase the stock of a retiring member. However, even with a mandatory retirement of sixty-five, there is no guarantee that any stock will be available when a wrestler retires. Most *rikishi*, therefore, make arrangements for acquiring stock long before they leave active wrestling. Exceptions are occasionally made to the rigid elder system, however. A rule allows *yokozuna* to become temporary elders, for five years, during which time they can try to acquire the necessary stock to make their status permanent. And two outstanding *yokozuna* of recent years, Taiho and Kitanoumi, were both accorded the status of one-generation elders (that is, the positions will be abolished upon their deaths, leaving the number at 105). The same status has already been promised to Chiyonofuji.

Only an elder in the Sumo Association is allowed to run a stable. Thus, there could theoretically be 105 stables, although, as we have seen, there are only about a third that number. One of the newest is the Azumazeki stable, opened by the former Takamiyama after he retired in 1985. Although Hawaiian-born Jesse Kuhaulua (Takamiyama's original name) never attained the rank of *yokozuna*, he was tremendously popular with the fans, and stands as the best example of the successful integration of a foreigner into Japan's traditional sport. It was Jesse who recruited the top non-Japanese wrestling today, Konishiki. Chiyonofuji is also said to be planning to open his own stable; he has used some of his millions to purchase a 3,500-square-foot plot for the purpose.

In spite of the popular wisdom, many sumo wrestlers do go on to live long and active lives. A study of wrestlers active in the 1920s indicated an average lifespan of sixty-four years, longer than that of the male population as a whole of the same generation. The most serious health problems faced by retired wrestlers are a tendency to diabetes and heart trouble, due to their years of packing away the *chanko-nabe*, rice, saké, and beer. They also typically have problems with tendons and lower joints, particularly the knees. For these reasons, most wrestlers begin to shed weight as soon as they retire. But they don't necessarily give up the *chanko-nabe*. Many of the lesser-ranked *rikishi* go into the restaurant business, and specialize in the dish that they have been preparing and eating all their lives.

CHAPTER 13

The Lure of Sumo

Why watch? Answers to this question are as varied as the interests and temperaments of the fans. Here, I will confine discussion to why a *foreigner* might enjoy sumo; to the Japanese, its pleasures are no mystery.

At its most basic level, sumo presents the typical attractions of stadium spectator sports. Fans can relax, eat, drink, and enjoy the spectacle of highly trained athletes in competition. The price of the cheapest ticket, as mentioned previously, is less than that for a Tokyo movie theater, and it will buy the serious fan eight hours of action. Moreover, after a bit of reading—of daily newspaper coverage, specialist magazines, or books such as this—fans will begin to recognize and cheer on their favorites. As with any sport, interest mounts as one's knowledge of it increases.

However, even if a day at the Kokugikan does not elicit wild enthusiasm from the foreigner, it does from the Japanese fans, and this is a perfectly valid reason to go join in the fun. To learn about a people and their culture, it is both useful and interesting to find out what excites and impresses them. The excitement, I might add, is contagious—when a *yokozuna* hoists his leg high and brings it crashing to the ground during his *dohyo-iri*, when a dozen or so banners indicating extra prize money are paraded around the ring, when a sure loser turns the tables at the last second with a skillful *utchari*—in such moments it is impossible not to be caught up in the spirit of the crowd.

Another big draw of sumo is its ritual, an element which has largely been stripped from sports in the West. The president may throw out the first baseball of the season, and we light the Olympic torch before those games begin, but, generally, after a perfunctory national anthem we're ready to get on with the program. However, something seems lacking in this modern, businesslike approach to fun, something that we rediscover in the stately, ceremonial approach to combat we see in sumo. Even the most insensitive and uninterested observer of the *dohyo-iri* can feel the power of a tradition developed through centuries of the intermingling of sport with religious rite.

At the same time, it is the ritual that is often accused of slowing down sumo, to a pace that is unacceptably sluggish for action-oriented foreigners. Frankly, I find this reasoning somewhat suspect; if a videotape of an American football game is edited to remove everything but the plays—the action between the snap of the ball and the referee's whistle—a typical three-hour game can be viewed in fifteen minutes. Moreover, in sumo, unlike in American football, the contest begins even before opponents clash, in the *shikiri-naoshi*, a subtle psychological duel, but one that is as important as the physical struggle in determining the outcome of a bout.

My personal advice to anyone curious about sumo is simply to go and watch it; I have no vested interest in winning converts to the sport. However, I cannot leave the subject without offering my own assessment of its allure.

Throughout history, people have been fascinated by physical competition; indeed, it is this intrinsic characteristic of our race that has given rise to sport. This competition can be divided into two main types: team contests, which emphasize group coordination, and individual contests, which emphasize personal strength and will. I suggest that it is the latter type that most enthralls us—we may go to watch the team but we identify with the individual player.

The ultimate contest then, is two individuals battling each other for the fruits of victory. Countless variants of this scenario have been acted out, throughout history and in many lands. The stakes have differed—a treasure, a woman, a title, a life; and so have the rules and equipment—from fists and stones to lances and dueling pistols. But the essential goal and method have remained the same: to win by besting one's opponent. Sumo is the traditional Japanese version of this contest. But when we compare it carefully with other versions, we find that it excels on three counts.

First of all, sumo is civilized. Unlike boxing, for example, in which the goal is essentially to damage one's opponent until he can no longer fight, the *rikishi* does not seek to injure his rival. Drawing even a small amount of blood is cause for concern that the ritual purity of the proceedings has been violated.

Secondly, sumo is basic, elemental. Opponents meet each other armed with only the skill and strength developed through rigorous discipline and practice, unencumbered by weapons, padding, helmets or other protective gear. And the rules are simplicity itself—the seventy-odd variant holds notwithstanding, a wrestler must put his opponent down or out. No warning whistles, no mandatory eight count, no penalty points, no double faults, no time outs, no fines, no free throws, no loss of a down—the *rikishi* wins or loses in a flashing display of strength and skill that is the culmination of years of physical and psychological conditioning.

Finally, sumo is intense. This is a difficult point to make with the skeptical foreigner, who feels that a whole lot of time is wasted between short bursts of action. Admittedly, a little investment in time and interest is required before one becomes attuned to the rhythm of the sport, the wave of excitement that crests with each victory, the crests reaching higher and higher as the afternoon progresses. In such circumstances, rather than disappoint, the rapidity and finality of the clashes serve to underscore the intensity. Each win in sumo is like the game-saving basket at the buzzer, the go-ahead run in the bottom of the ninth, the clearing of the bar on the third and final try.

Of course, the men of sumo and the arena in which

they contend are adorned with trappings of ritual significance, and an understanding of the pageantry and symbolism can add immeasurably to one's enjoyment. But neither should these be allowed to obscure the fundamental dynamic of the sport—two *rikishi* face each other in a ring; *two* cannot be in the ring—a formula breathtaking in its simplicity, and, need I say it?—quintessentially Japanese.

Chanko-nabe Restaurants

At the following restaurants you can sample *chanko-nabe*, a delicious one-pot meal of meat or fish and vegetables that is the staple food of sumo wrestlers. *Chanko-nabe* can be eaten in any season, but is a special treat on cold winter evenings. Reservations are recommended.

ICHINOTANI
2-10-2 Soto-Kanda
Chiyoda-ku
Tel: 251-8500

HAMARIKI
2-14-5 Takadanobaba
Shinjuku-ku
Tel: 200-2901

KAWASAKI
2-13-1 Ryogoku, Sumida-ku
Tel: 631-2529

NARUYAMA
3-9-2 Kudan Minami
Chiyoda-ku
Tel: 261-1632

DAIKIRIN
1-1-11 Nezu, Bunkyo-ku
Tel: 823-5998

KIYOKUNI
2-24-13 Koishikawa
Bunkyo-ku
Tel: 816-5544

116 · CHANKO-NABE RESTAURANTS

KITASEUMI
1-21-22 Nishi-Koiwa
Edogawa-ku
Tel: 672-7393

TOMOEGATA
2-17-6 Ryogoku
Sumida-ku
Tel: 632-5600

TAMAKATSU
3-2-12 Negishi, Taito-ku
Tel: 872-8712

YOSHIBA
4-8-11 Ginza, Chuo-ku
Tel: 567-4481

FUTAGODAKE
3-58-1 Minami-Asagaya
Suginami-ku
Tel: 336-7527

FURIWAKE
3-35-15 Yushima
Bunkyo-ku
Tel: 836-5888

Addresses of Sumo Beya

Foreigners are often welcome to become members of a wrestler's *koen-kai* (supporters group). To join, write to the wrestler's stable at the address below (in Japanese). Visits to stables are also possible, but should be arranged in advance in the same manner.

AJIGAWA
1-7-4 Mori
Koto-ku, Tokyo 135

ASAHIYAMA
4-14-21 Kita-Kasai
Edogawa-ku, Tokyo 134

AZUMAZEKI
4-6-4 Higashi-Komagata
Sumida-ku, Tokyo 130

DEWANOUMI
2-3-15 Ryogoku
Sumida-ku, Tokyo 130

FUJISHIMA
3-10-6 Honcho
Nakano-ku, Tokyo 164

FUTAGOYAMA
3-25-10 Narita-Higashi
Suginami-ku, Tokyo 166

HANAREGOMA
3-12-7 Asagaya-Minami
Suginami-ku, Tokyo 166

ISEGAHAMA
5-7-14 Hakusan
Bunkyo-ku, Tokyo 112

ISENOUMI
3-8-80 Harue-cho
Edogawa-ku, Tokyo 132

IZUTSU
2-2-7 Ryogoku
Sumida-ku, Tokyo 130

KAGAMIYAMA
8-16-1 Kita-Koiwa
Edogawa-ku, Tokyo 133

KASUGANO
1-7-11 Ryogoku
Sumida-ku, Tokyo 130

KASUGAYAMA
1-10-14 Saga
Koto-ku, Tokyo 135

KATAONAMI
1-33-9 Ishiwara
Sumida-ku, Tokyo 130

KISO
2-35-21 Hongo
Bunkyo-ku, Tokyo 113

KITANOUMI
2-10-11 Kiyosumi
Koto-ku, Tokyo 135

KOKONOE
1-16-1 Kamezawa
Sumida-ku, Tokyo 130

KUMAGATANI
1-6-28 Minami-Koiwa
Edogawa-ku, Tokyo 133

MAGAKI
3-8-1 Kamezawa
Sumida-ku, Tokyo 130

MICHINOKU
3-13-14 Hirai
Edogawa-ku, Tokyo 132

MIHOGASEKI
3-2-12 Chitose
Sumida-ku, Tokyo 130

MINATO
2-20-10 Shibanakata
Kawaguchi-shi
Saitama-ken 333

MIYAGINO
4-16-3 Midori
Sumida-ku, Tokyo 130

MUSASHIGAWA
3-2-9 Hirano
Koto-ku, Tokyo 135

NISHONOSEKI
4-17-1 Ryogaku
Sumida-ku, Tokyo 130

ONARUTO
2-22-14 Kitakata
Ichikawa-shi
Chiba-ken 272

OSHIMA
3-5-3 Ryogoku
Sumida-ku, Tokyo 130

OSHIOGAWA
2-17-7 Kiba
Koto-ku, Tokyo 135

OYAMA
5-35-13 Higashi-Koiwa
Edogawa-ku, Tokyo 133

SADOGATAKE
4-18-13 Taihei
Sumida-ku, Tokyo 130

TAIHO
2-8-3 Kiyosumi
Koto-ku, Tokyo 135

TAKADAGAWA
2-1-15 Ichioe
Edogawa-ku, Tokyo 132

TAKASAGO
1-22-5 Yanagibashi
Taito-ku, Tokyo 111

TATSUNAMI
3-26-2 Ryogoku
Sumida-ku, Tokyo 130

TATSUTAGAWA
4-7-11 Ryogoku
Sumida, Tokyo 130

TOKITSUKAZE
3-15-3 Ryogoku
Sumida-ku, Tokyo 130

TOMOZUNA
1-20-7 Mori
Koto-ku, Tokyo 135

WAKAMATSU
2-10-8 Ryogoku
Sumida-ku, Tokyo 130

Information about sumo (in Japanese) is available from:

Nihon Sumo Kyokai
(Japan Sumo Association)
1-3-28 Yokoami
Sumida-ku, Tokyo 130
623-5111

Glossary of Sumo Terms

akeni: lacquered, wickerware trunk used by *sekitori* to carry their sumo gear

banzuke: ranking list of wrestlers for a tournament
basho: sumo tournament
basho-teate: an allowance given wrestlers for appearing in a tournament
beya: sumo "stable," where wrestlers live and train
bintsuke: scented hair pomade worn by wrestlers
butsukari-geiko: practice in which smaller wrestlers try to push larger wrestlers from the ring

chanko-nabe: stew eaten daily by *rikishi*
chikara-gami: "paper of strength," used by wrestlers to wipe their lips before bouts
chikara-mizu: "water of strength," used by wrestlers to rinse their mouths prior to bouts
chon-mage: rikishi hairstyle consisting of a simple topknot

danpatsu-shiki: hair-cutting ceremony marking a *rikishi's* retirement

122 · GLOSSARY

de-geiko: practice competition between members of different *beya*
dohyo: sumo ring
dohyo-iri: ring-entering ceremony
dohyo-matsuri: ceremony to inagurate and purify a ring

gino-sho: prize awarded for displaying excellent technique during a tournament
gohei: white, zigzag paper strips that hang from the front of a *yokozuna's* belt
gyoji: sumo referee

hataki-komi: sidestepping an opponent's charge and slapping him down
hidari-yotsu: gripping an opponent's belt with the left hand inside his

jonidan: of the six divisions of sumo, second from the bottom
jonokuchi: the lowest division of sumo
jungyo: exhibition tours that follow each of the grand tournaments
juryo: of the six divisions of sumo, second from the top

kachi-koshi: tournament performance resulting in a majority of wins
kanto-sho: prize awarded for displaying fighting spirit in a tournament
kawaigatte: the slapping or hitting of a junior *rikishi* to inspire fighting spirit
keiko: general term for sumo training exercises
kensho: prize for winning a bout
kesho-mawashi: elaborately embroidered apron worn during the ring-entering ceremony
kimari-te: the various winning techniques of sumo
kinboshi: "gold star," awarded an ordinary *makunouchi* wrestler for defeating a *yokozuna*
koen-kai: supporters group or fan club of a *sekitori* or stable

Kokugikan: the sumo stadium at Ryogoku (or one of two previous halls of the same name)

komusubi: junior champion, second class; lowest of the *sanyaku* ranks

kote-nage: using a grip on an opponent's forearm to throw him down

kubi-nage: using an arm around an opponent's neck to throw him down

Kyokai: short for Nihon Sumo Kyokai, the Japan Sumo Association

mae-zumo: designating wrestlers and bouts below the six regular divisions

maegashira: tournament ranking held by *makunouchi* wrestlers who are not *sanyaku* or *yokozuna*

make-koshi: tournament performance resulting in a majority of losses

makunouchi: the highest of the six divisions of sumo

makushita: of the six divisions of sumo, fourth from the bottom

matawari: seated splits with the chest pressed to the ground

mawashi: canvas or silk belt worn by *rikishi*

migi-yotsu: gripping an opponent's belt with the right hand inside his

mono-ii: conference of judges following a disputed bout

moro-zashi: gripping an opponent's belt with both hands inside his

moshiai-geiko: practice competition in which a winner takes on challengers until he loses

o-icho-mage: "ginkgo-leaf" hairstyle worn by *sekitori* for tournaments and formal occasions

oshi-dashi: technique of winning by pushing out an opponent

oshi-taoshi: technique of winning by pushing down an opponent

oyakata: title used with the name of an elder in the Japan Sumo Association

ozeki: champion; top *sanyaku* rank, just below *yokozuna*

rikishi: sumo wrestler of any division

sagari: cloth strip hung with an odd number of stiffened silk cords, worn by wrestlers

sanban-geiko: practice in which two men of different divisions fight multiple bouts

sandanme: of sumo's six divisions, third from the bottom

sanyaku: the three top ranks below *yokozuna*

sekitori: sumo wrestler of one of the top two divisions

sekiwake: junior champion, first class; second of the *sanyaku* ranks

shikiri-naoshi: repeated toeing the mark, squatting, and staring prior to *sekitori* bouts

shiko: training exercise in which a leg is lifted high and stamped down hard

shikona: special fighting name taken by a *rikishi*

shimpan: sumo judge

shiranui: style of *yokozuna* ring-entering ceremony devised by Shiranui Koemon

shitate-nage: throwing an opponent using an inner grip on the belt

shukun-sho: prize awarded for an outstanding tournament performance

soto-gake: tripping an opponent by wrapping a leg around his leg from the outside

sumotori: sumo wrestler, usually one of the lower four divisions

tachi-ai: the simultaneous, initial charge of *rikishi* that opens a bout

tachi-mori: rikishi who carries a *yokozuna's* sword during the ring-entering ceremony

tate-gyoji: the head referee

tawara: straw bales sunk into the dirt of the *dohyo*, forming a circle and square

tegata: a *rikishi's* palm print, usually printed in red and autographed, for fans

teppo: training excerise involving slapping a wooden pole with the open hand

tokoyama: professional sumo hairdresser
tori-naoshi: a rematch following a disputed bout
tsukebito: junior wrestler appointed as an attendant to a senior *rikishi*
tsuki-dashi: slapping or thrusting an opponent out of the ring
tsuki-taoshi: slapping or thrusting an opponent down inside the ring
tsuna: white ceremonial rope belt, the mark of the *yokozuna* rank
tsuppari: slapping or thrusting with the open hands
tsuri-dashi: lifting an opponent up and out of the ring
tsuri-otoshi: lifting an opponent and then forcing him down
tsuri-harai: literally "dew-sweeper," an attendant to a *yokozuna* during his *dohyo-iri*

uchi-gake: tripping an opponent by wrapping a leg around his leg from the inside
unryu: style of *yokozuna* ring-entering ceremony devised by Unryu Hisakichi
utchari: technique in which an apparent loser turns and throws down his opponent
uwate-nage: using an outside belt grip to throw an opponent down

yobidashi: ring announcer
yokozuna: grand champion, the top rank in sumo
yori-kiri: using a grip on an opponent's belt to force him out of the ring
yori-taoshi: using a grip on an opponent's belt to force him out of the ring and down
yumitori-shiki: bow-twirling ceremony that concludes a tournament day
yusho: tournament championship

zensho-yusho: tournament victory won with a perfect record

Other Titles in the Tuttle Library of Martial Arts

AIKIDO AND THE DYNAMIC SPHERE
by Adele Westbrook and Oscar Ratti

Aikido is a Japanese method of self-defense that can be used against any form of attack and that is also a way of harmonizing all of one's vital powers into an integrated, energy-filled whole.

BLACK BELT KARATE *by Jordan Roth*

A no-frills, no-holds barred handbook on the fundamentals of modern karate. Over 800 techniques and exercises and more than 1,850 photographs reveal the speed and power inherent in properly taught karate.

THE ESSENCE OF OKINAWAN KARATE-DO
by Shoshin Nagamine

"Nagamine's book will awaken in all who read it a new understanding of the Okinawan open-handed martial art."

—Gordon Warner
Kendo 7th dan, renshi

THE NINJA AND THEIR SECRET FIGHTING ART
by Stephen K. Hayes

The *ninja* were the elusive spies and assassins of feudal Japan. This book explains their lethal system of unarmed combat, unique weapons, and mysterious techniques of stealth.

SECRET FIGHTING ARTS OF THE WORLD
by John F. Gilbey

> Suppressed for centuries, twenty of the world's most secretly guarded fighting techniques are vividly described in this amazing volume.

SECRETS OF THE SAMURAI *by Oscar Ratti and Adele Westbrook*

> A definitive study of the martial arts of feudal Japan, illustrating the techniques, weapons, strategies, and principles of combat that made the Japanese samurai a terrible foe.

STICKFIGHTING: A PRACTICAL GUIDE TO SELF-PROTECTION *by Evan S. Baltazzi*

> Over 400 photographs illustrate in a systematic way the simple, versatile, and comprehensive approach to a method of self-protection accessible to all.

THIS IS KENDO *by Junzo Sasamori and Gordon Warner*

> The first book in English to describe the origin and history of kendo, its basic principles and techniques, its etiquette, and its relation to Zen. A must for any serious martial artist.

THE WAY OF KARATE *by George E. Mattson*

> A fully illustrated explanation of the Okinawan style of karate; an indispensable introduction to its true nature and basic techniques, with emphasis on its value in both training and self-defense.